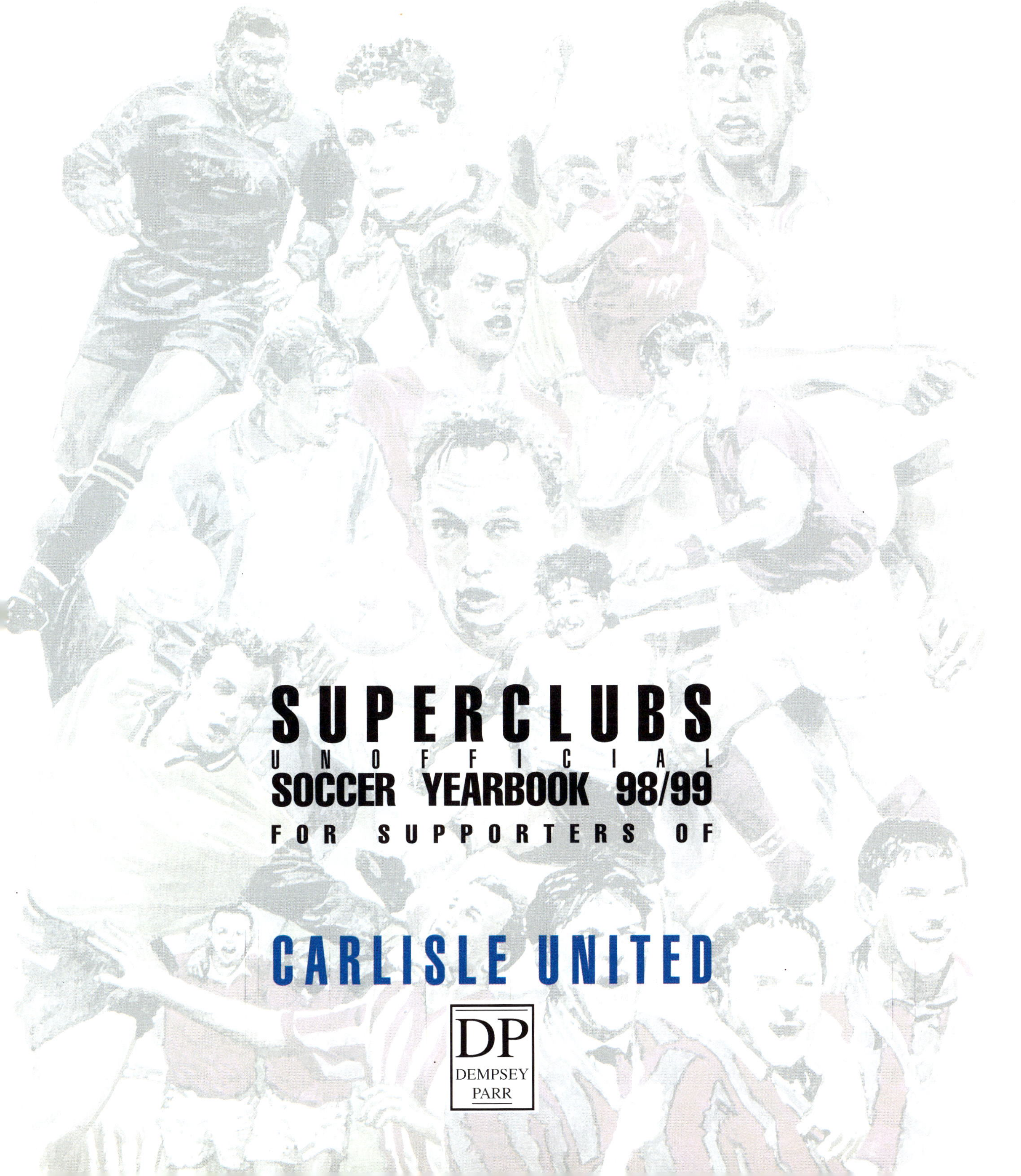

SUPERCLUBS

UNOFFICIAL

SOCCER YEARBOOK 98/99

FOR SUPPORTERS OF

CARLISLE UNITED

DP
DEMPSEY
PARR

First published in Great Britain in 1998 by
Dempsey Parr
13 Whiteladies Road
Clifton
Bristol BS8 1PB

ISBN: 1840840781

Produced for Dempsey Parr by
Prima Creative Services

Editorial director Roger Kean
Managing editor Tim Smith (Content E.D.B.)
Contributing authors
Steve Bradley
Jim Drewett (Deadline Features)
Steve Farragher
Sam Johnstone
Alex Leith (Deadline Features)
Rex Nash
Russell Smith
Tim Smith

Cover background and illustrations by Oliver Frey

Design and repro by Prima Creative Services

Printed and bound in Italy by L.E.G.O., Vicenza

Picture Acknowledgements
The publisher would like to thank the staff of Allsport and Action Images for their unstinting help and all the other libraries, newspapers and photographers who have made this edition possible. All pictures are credited alongside the photograph.

Action Images

SUPERCLUBS
UNOFFICIAL
SOCCER YEARBOOK 98/99
FOR SUPPORTERS OF

CARLISLE UNITED

CONTENTS

STATISTICS

The first club outside London to install floodlighting, Carlisle are also the most isolated British League club – their nearest 'neighbours' being Newcastle, some 58 miles away. The Blues' proudest moment came in August 1974 when, having just won promotion to the old First Division, they sat on top of the table. But no team can live on memories – especially those of last season. The wake-up call has been sounded, the fans are hungry for a return to top-flight footy, now it's up to the team to perform in 1998-99.

Date Formed: 1903
Date Entered Football League: 1928
Former Names: Shaddongate United
Official Nickname: The Cumbrians
Other Nicknames: The Blues

MANAGERS SINCE JOINED LEAGUE:

George Bristow	(1913–30)	Ian MacFarlane	(1970–72)
Billy Hampson	(1930–33)	Alan Ashman	(1972–75)
Bill Clarke	(1933–35)	Dick Young	(1975–76)
Robert Kelly	(1935–36)	Bobby Moncur	(1976–80)
Fred Westgarth	(1936–38)	Martin Harvey	(1980)
David Taylor	(1938–40)	Bob Stokoe	(1980–85)
Howard Harkness	(1940–45)	Bryan 'Pop' Robson	(1985)
Bill Clark	(1945–46)	Bob Stokoe	(1985–86)
Ivor Broadis	(1946–49)	Harry Gregg	(1986–87)
Bill Shankly	(1949–51)	Cliff Middlemass	(1987–91)
Fred Emery	(1951–58)	Aidan McCaffery	(1991–92)
Andy Beattie	(1958–60)	David McCreery	(1992–93)
Ivor Powell	(1960–63)	Mick Wadsworth	(1993–6)
Alan Ashman	(1963–67)	Mervyn Day	(1996–97)
Tim Ward	(1967–68)	John Halpin/David Wilkes	
Bob Stokoe	(1968–70)		(1997–)

ACTION IMAGES

A glory moment for the Cumbrians: Andy Couzens celebrates his goal against Spurs in the Coca-Cola Cup 2nd round. The Brunton Park faithful will want a lot more of this in the new term

CLUB HONOURS

Division Three Champions
1965, 1995
Division Three Runners-Up
1982
Division Four Runners-Up
1964
Auto Windscreen Shield Runners-Up 1995 (April 23rd, Wembley)
Carlisle United v Birmingham City 0–1

Auto Windscreen Shield Winners 1997 (April 20th, Wembley)
Carlisle United v Colchester 0–0 (4–3 on penalties)

Chairman: M. Knighton
Club Sponsors: Eddie Stobart Ltd

Record Attendance: 27,500 against Birmingham City, FA Cup Third Round, January 5th 1957 and against Middlesbrough, FA Cup Fifth Round, February 7th 1970

Warren Aspinall outruns Spurs' Sol Campbell, 30/9/97

ACTION IMAGES

Stadiums: 1903–05 Milholme Bank
1905–09 Devonshire Park
1909– Brunton Park

Address: Brunton Park, Warwick Road, Carlisle, Cumbria CA1 1LL

Capacity: 17,300 (28,000 target capacity)

Stands: Warwick Road End, East Stand, Petteril End, Pirelli Family Stand

Prices: Adults £8, £11
Children £5, £6 (second accompanied child £3)
OAPs £5, £6

Season ticket prices: Adults £176–£242
OAPs £110–£132; Children £110–£132 (second accompanied child £66)

Parking facilities: Club car park for 1,500 vehicles, access in St Aidan's Road. Restricted street parking.

PITCH DIMENSIONS

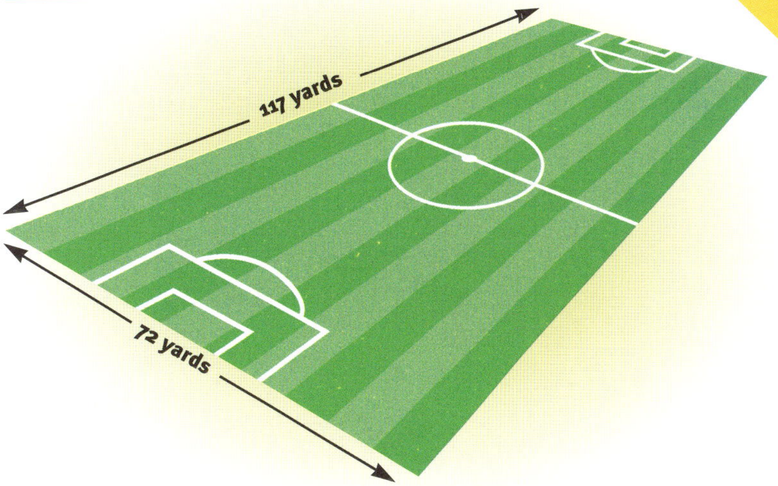

BEST PUB

The Beehive, Warwick Road – extremely popular matchday pub close to the ground.

Owen Archdeacon in action last season

PETE NORTON PHOTOGRAPHY

Preferred team formation: 5–3–2
Biggest rivals: Preston North End, Blackpool and Burnley

Programme: Blues Review
Programme Editor: Jim Thoburn
Programme Price: £1.20
Bus routes to stadium: Carlisle Citadel Station closest railway link. Bus number 70 to Durranhill from the town centre.

FANZINES

Hit The Bar, 14 Hartland Road, Friern Barnet, London, N11 3JJ

Cumberland Sausage, 4 Wetheral Street, Carlisle, Cumbria, CA2 5UP

What The Fox Going On?, 68 Richardson Street, Carlisle CA2 6AA

Land of Sheep and Glory, Tarbrax, Wreay, Carlisle, CA4 0RL

CONTACT NUMBERS

(Telephone Code 01228)

- Main number 526237
- Fax 530138
- Commercial dept 524014
- Clubcall 0891 121 632

LEADING PLAYERS

Will Varty finds hanging onto Chris Armstrong one way of stopping a goal. What the Cumbrians need now is to make their own opportunities, and with the right mix of youth and experience, it can't be a long haul back to Division Two

Action Images

1997/98 SEASON TOP 10 GOALSCORERS

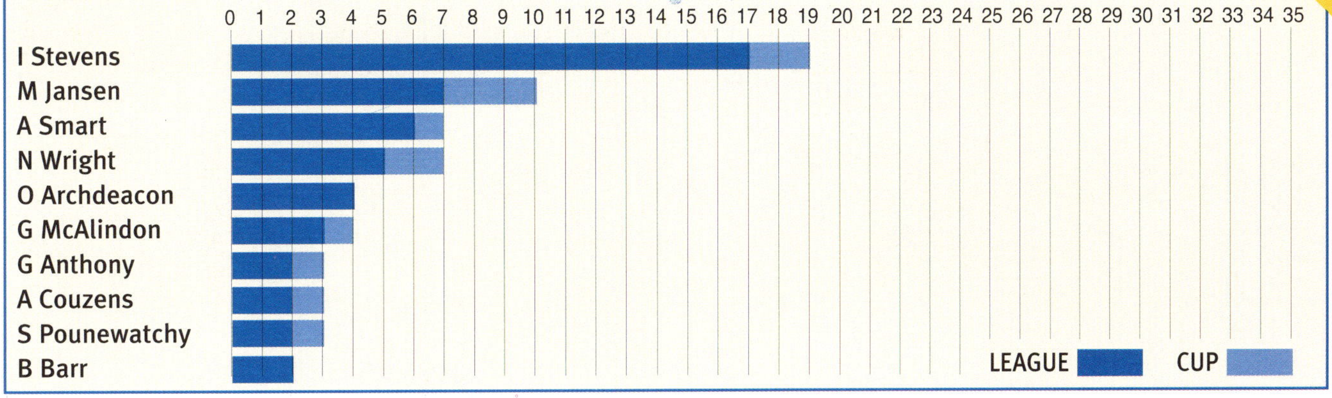

MOST LEAGUE APPEARANCES

PLAYER	APPEARANCES	SUBSTITUTE	GOALS
1 Tony Caig	46	0	0
2 Will Varty	43	1	1
3 Billy Barr	39	0	2
4 Stephane Pounewatchy	39	0	2
5 Ian Stevens	33	4	17
6 Richard Prokas	33	1	0
7 Gareth McAlindon	16	12	3
8 Andy Couzens	18	9	2
9 Graham Anthony	25	0	2
10 Nick Wright	25	0	5
11 Matt Jansen	22	1	7
12 Scott Dobie	9	14	1
13 Tony Hopper	16	3	0
14 Owen Archdeacon	18	0	4
15 Warren Aspinall	18	0	0
16 Allan Smart	16	0	6
17 Jeff Thorpe	12	2	0
18 Ron Wallwork	10	0	1
19 Tom Harrison	6	4	0
20 Paul Boertien	8	1	0

PLAYER STATISTICS

Record transfer fee paid:
David Reeves – £121,000 from Notts County, December 1993

Record transfer fee received:
Matt Jansen, £1,000,000 (rising to £2,000,000 with appearances) from Crystal Palace, February 1988

Oldest player: Bryan 'Pop' Robson, 39 years and 321 days against Shrewsbury Town, September 28th 1985

Youngest player: Rory Delap, 16 years and 306 days against Scarborough, May 8th 1993

International captains:
None

Most capped player:
Eric Welsh, 4, Northern Ireland (1966–67)

SQUAD

TONY CAIG
DOB: 11/4/74
Position: Goalkeeper
Usual shirt number: 1
Joined club: July 1992 from trainee
League Games played: 186
League Goals scored: 0
International caps: 0
League Debut: 3/10/92 v Halifax (H)

GEORGE DIXON
DOB: 24/10/78
Position: Goalkeeper
Usual shirt number: 1
Joined club: March 1996 from trainee
League Games played: 0
League Goals scored: 0
International caps: 0
League Debut: Not made yet

PAUL BOERTIEN
DOB: 20/1/79
Position: Defender
Usual shirt number: 3
Joined club: May 1997 from trainee
League Games played: 9
League Goals scored: 0
International caps: 0
League Debut: 4/10/97 v Walsall (A)

ROB BOWMAN
DOB: 21/11/75
Position: Defender
Usual shirt number: 2
Joined club: August 1997 from Rotherham United
League Games played: 7
League Goals scored: 1
International caps: 0
League Debut: 11/10/97 v Burnley (A)

ACTION IMAGES

Clean sheets will be another key to success in 1998-99

TONY HOPPER
DOB: 31/5/76
Position: Defender
Usual shirt number: 2
Joined club: July 1994 from trainee
League Games played: 50
League Goals scored: 1
International caps: 0
League Debut: May 1993

STEPHANE POUNEWATCHY

DOB: 10/2/68
Position: Defender
Usual shirt number: 6
Joined club: August 1996 from Gueugnon
League Games played: 81
League Goals scored: 2
International caps: 0
League Debut: 17/8/96 v Doncaster Rovers (A)

RICHARD PROKAS

DOB: 22/1/76
Position: Defender
Usual shirt number: 3
Joined club: July 1994 from trainee
League Games played: 106
League Goals scored: 2
International caps: 0
League Debut: 20/8/94 v Wigan Athletic (H)

LEE TAYLOR

DOB: 12/9/77
Position: Defender
Usual shirt number: 6
Joined club: August 1996 from trainee
League Games played: 0
League Goals scored: 0
International caps: 0
League Debut: Not made yet

JEFF THORPE

DOB: 17/11/72
Position: Defender
Usual shirt number: 3
Joined club: July 1991 from trainee
League Games played: 150
League Goals scored: 6
International caps: 0
League Debut: 25/10/90 v Scarborough (A)

PETE NORTON PHOTOGRAPHY

Richard Prokas, starting his fifth season with the Cumbrians

The right mix of youth...: 20-year-old Matt Jansen, only in his second full season, scored seven league and three cup goals in his first

Pete Norton Photography

GRAHAM ANTHONY

DOB: 9/8/75
Position: Midfielder
Usual shirt number: 7
Joined club: November 1997 from Plymouth Argyle
League Games played: 25
League Goals scored: 2
International caps: 0
League Debut: 29/11/97 v Bristol City (H)

BILLY BARR

DOB: 21/1/69
Position: Midfielder
Usual shirt number: 4
Joined club: July 1997 from Crewe Alexandra
League Games played: 39
League Goals scored: 2
International caps: 0
League Debut: 9/8/97 v Southend (A)

ANDY COUZENS

DOB: 4/6/75
Position: Midfielder
Usual shirt number: 8
Joined club: July 1997 from Leeds United
League Games played: 18
League Goals scored: 2
International caps: 0
League Debut: 23/8/97 v Bristol Rovers

WILL VARTY

DOB: 1/10/76
Position: Defender
Usual shirt number: 5
Joined club: July 1995 from trainee
League Games played: 76
League Goals scored: 1
International caps: 0
League Debut: 17/8/96 v Doncaster Rovers (A)

KEVIN SANDWITH

DOB: 30/4/78
Position: Midfielder
Usual shirt number: 5
Joined club: October 1996 from trainee
League Games played: 1
League Goals scored: 0
International caps: 0
League Debut: 2/5/98 v Luton Town (A)

PETE NORTON PHOTOGRAPHY

And at 19, Scott Dobie is another young striker whose promise Brunton Park eagerly awaits

GARETH McALINDON

DOB: 6/4/77
Position: Striker
Usual shirt number: 10
Joined club: July 1995 from Newcastle United
League Games played: 43
League Goals scored: 5
International caps: 0
League Debut: 21/10/95 v Bradford City (H)

ALLAN SMART

DOB: 8/7/74
Position: Striker
Usual shirt number: 9
Joined club: November 1995 (on loan) and October 1996 from Preston North End
League Games played: 48
League Goals scored: 16
International caps: 0
League Debut: 26/11/95 v Wycombe Wanderers (H)

SCOTT DOBIE

DOB: 10/10/78
Position: Striker
Usual shirt number: 10
Joined club: April 1997 from trainee
League Games played: 25
League Goals scored: 2
International caps: 0
League Debut: 29/4/97 v Rochdale (H)

IAN STEVENS

DOB: 21/10/66
Position: Striker
Usual shirt number: 9
Joined club: May 1997 from Shrewsbury Town
League Games played: 37
League Goals scored: 17
International caps: 0
League Debut: 25/10/97 v York City (A)

MATT JANSEN

DOB: 20/10/77
Position: Striker
Usual shirt number: 10
Joined club: January 1996 from trainee
League Games played: 41
League Goals scored: 8
International caps: 0
League Debut: 5/10/96 v Mansfield

NICK WRIGHT

DOB: 15/10/75
Position: Striker
Usual shirt number: 2
Joined club: November 1997 from Derby County
League Games played: 25
League Goals scored: 5
International caps: 0
League Debut: 29/11/97 v Bristol City (H)

ALL-TIME RECORDS

1997/98 SEASON FINAL POSITIONS

POINTS 10 20 30 40 50 60 70 80 90 100 200 300 400 500

Club	Points	Goals	Position in Division Three at start of 1998/99 season	Average position by points in the league since joining	Average position by goals in the league since joining
Barnet	430	392	7	90	90
Brentford	3508	4575	1	44	51
Brighton & Hove Alb	3461	4563	23	48	52
Cambridge United	1491	1638	16	86	86
Cardiff City	3200	4163	21	66	69
Carlisle United	2922	3968	3	76	74
Chester City	2808	3796	14	78	77
Darlington	3046	4339	19	72	63
Exeter City	3166	4295	15	68	66
Halifax Town	2723	3694	24	79	78
Hartlepool United	2999	4120	17	73	71
Hull City	3838	5089	22	32	33
Leyton Orient	3524	4587	11	41	49
Mansfield Town	2912	4002	12	77	73
Peterborough Utd	2104	2529	10	84	84
Plymouth Argyle	3465	5650	2	47	24
Rochdale	3067	4218	18	71	68
Rotherham United	3138	4356	9	69	62
Scarborough	639	647	6	89	89
Scunthorpe United	2447	2996	8	81	82
Shrewsbury Town	2344	2952	13	83	83
Southend United	3412	4586	4	53	50
Swansea City	3267	4408	20	63	61
Torquay United	2979	3948	5	74	74

3 Position in Division Three at start of 1998/99 season

92 Average position by points in the league since joining — includes 2 points for a win and 3 points for a win

92 Average position by goals in the league since joining

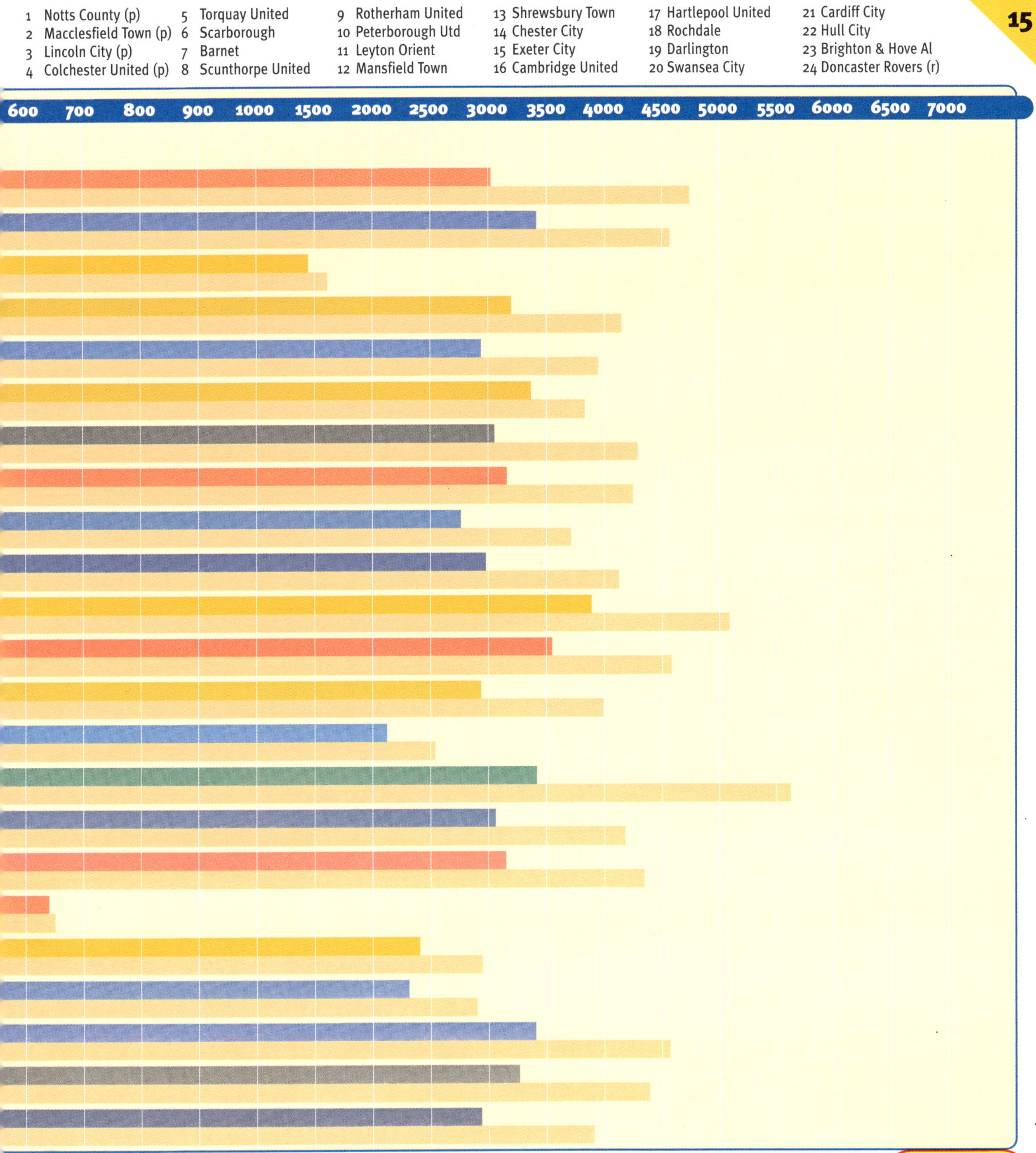

Carlisle United's total points since joining league 2922

Brunton Park: home of Carlisle United
AEROFILMS

SUPERCLUBS
UNOFFICIAL
SOCCER YEARBOOK 98/99

JULY 1998 – JUNE 1999 DIARY AND CLUB FIXTURES

Fixture dates are subject to change. FA Cup draws were not made at the time of going to press. Worthington Cup draws are given where known at press time.

THE STORY OF DIVISION THREE SOCCER IN THE 1997/98 SEASON

FOR SUPPORTERS OF
CARLISLE UNITED

DIVISION THREE CLUB ADDRESSES

BARNET
Underhill Stadium, Barnet Lane, Barnet, Herts, EN5 2BE
Main No: 0181 441 6932

BRIGHTON AND HOVE ALBION
188, Queens Road Brighton BN1 3XG
(Temporary ground Priestfield Stadium, Redfern Avenue, Gillingham, Kent ME7 4DD, with proposed move to Withdean Stadium during 1998/99 still unconfirmed as we go to press)
Main No: 01273 778 855

CAMBRIDGE UNITED
Abbey Stadium, Newmarket Road, Cambridge, CB5 8LN
Main No: 01223 566 500

CHESTER CITY
The Deva Stadium, Bumpers Lane, Chester, Cheshire, CH1 4LT
Main No: 01244 371 809

COLCHESTER UNITED
Layer Road Ground, Colchester, Essex, CO2 7JJ
Main No: 01206 508 800

DARLINGTON
Feethams Ground, Darlington, Co Durham, DL1 5JB
Main No: 01325 465 097

EXETER CITY
St James Park, Well Street, Exeter, Devon, EX4 6PX
Main No: 01392 254 073

HALIFAX
Shay Grounds, Halifax, HX1 2YS
Main No: 01422 345 543

HARTLEPOOL UNITED
The Victoria Ground, Clarence Road, Hartlepool, Cleveland, TS24 8BZ
Main No: 01429 272 584

HULL CITY
Boothferry Park, Boothferry Road, Hull, North Humberside, HU4 6EU
Main No: 01482 351119

LEYTON ORIENT
Leyton Stadium, Brisbane Road, Leyton, London, E10 5NE
Main No: 0181 926 1111

LINCOLN CITY
Sincil Bank, Lincoln, LN5 8LD
Main No: 01522 880 011

MACCLESFIELD TOWN
The Moss Rose Ground, London Road, Macclesfield Town, Cheshire, SK11 7SP
Main No: 01625 264 686

MANSFIELD TOWN
Field Mill Ground, Quarry Lane, Mansfield Notts, NG18 5DA
Main No: 01623 235 67

NOTTS COUNTY
County Ground, Meadow Lane, Nottingham, NG2 3HJ
Main No: 0115 952 9000

PETERBOROUGH UNITED
London Road Ground, Peterborough, PE2 8AL
Main No: 01733 563 947

ROCHDALE
Spotland, Sandy Lane, Rochdale, OL11 5DS
Main No: 01706 644 648

ROTHERHAM UNITED
Millmoor Ground, Rotherham, S60 1HR
Main No: 01709 512 434

SCARBOROUGH
The McCain Stadium, Seamer Road, Scarborough, YO12 4HF
Main No: 01723 375 094

SCUNTHORPE UNITED
Glanford Park, Scunthorpe, South Humberside, DN15 8TD
Main No: 01724 848 077

SHREWSBURY TOWN
Gay Meadow, Shrewsbury, Shropshire, SY2 6AB
Main No: 01743 360 111

SWANSEA CITY
Vetch Field, Swansea, SA1 3SU
Main No: 01792 474 114

TORQUAY UNITED
Plainmoor Road, Torquay, Devon, TQ1 3PS
Main No: 01803 328 666

ALL-CLUB LOCATIONS

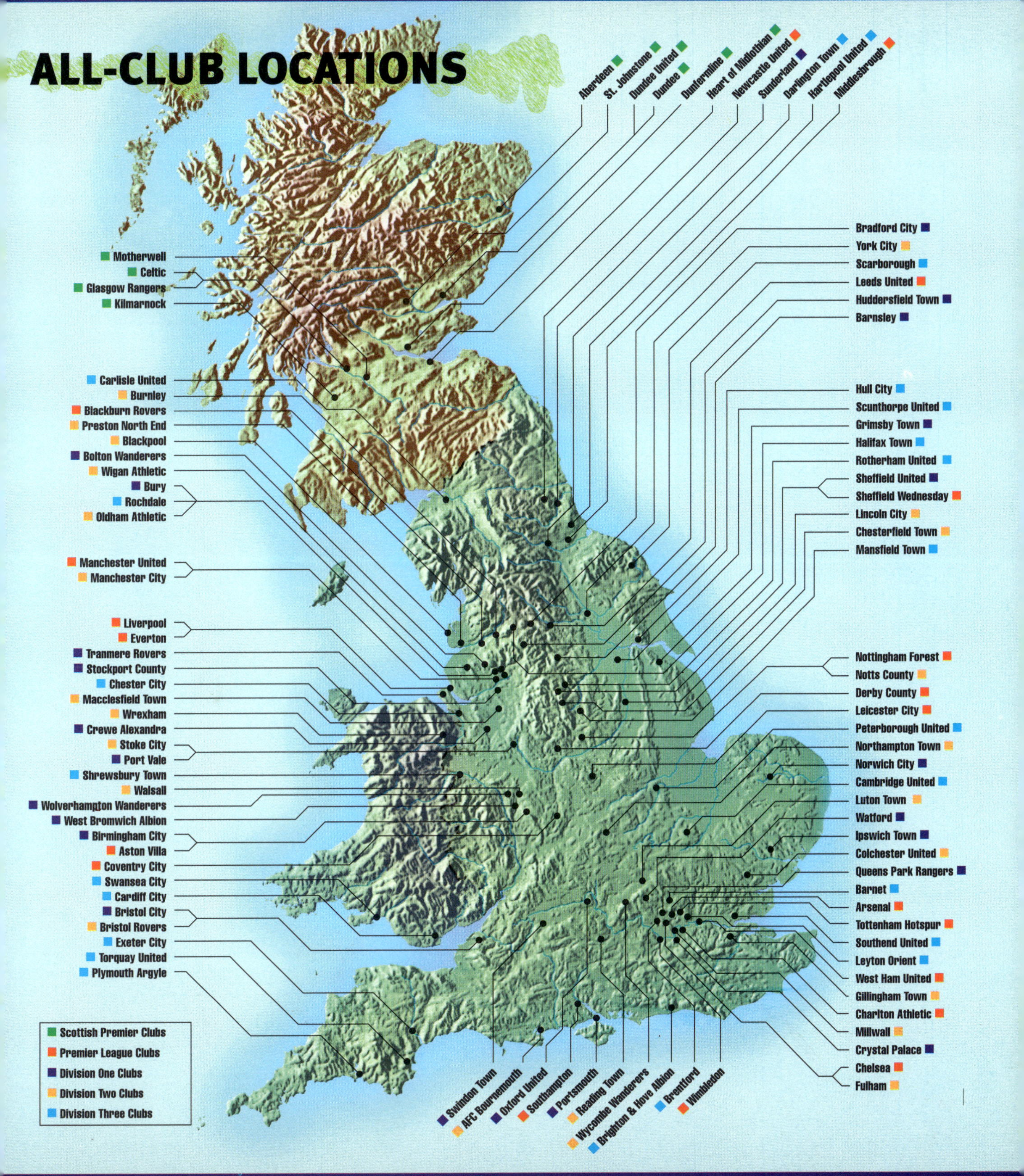

CALENDAR 1998

January

	M	T	W	T	F	S	S
1				1	2	3	4
2	5	6	7	8	9	10	11
3	12	13	14	15	16	17	18
4	19	20	21	22	23	24	25
5	26	27	28	29	30	31	

February

	M	T	W	T	F	S	S
5							1
6	2	3	4	5	6	7	8
7	9	10	11	12	13	14	15
8	16	17	18	19	20	21	22
9	23	24	25	26	27	28	

March

	M	T	W	T	F	S	S
9							1
10	2	3	4	5	6	7	8
11	9	10	11	12	13	14	15
12	16	17	18	19	20	21	22
13	23	24	25	26	27	28	29
14	30	31					

April

	M	T	W	T	F	S	S
14			1	2	3	4	5
15	6	7	8	9	10	11	12
16	13	14	15	16	17	18	19
17	20	21	22	23	24	25	26
18	27	28	29	30			

May

	M	T	W	T	F	S	S
18					1	2	3
19	4	5	6	7	8	9	10
20	11	12	13	14	15	16	17
21	18	19	20	21	22	23	24
22	25	26	27	28	29	30	31

June

	M	T	W	T	F	S	S
23	1	2	3	4	5	6	7
24	8	9	10	11	12	13	14
25	15	16	17	18	19	20	21
26	22	23	24	25	26	27	28
27	29	30					

July

	M	T	W	T	F	S	S
27			1	2	3	4	5
28	6	7	8	9	10	11	12
29	13	14	15	16	17	18	19
30	20	21	22	23	24	25	26
31	27	28	29	30	31		

August

	M	T	W	T	F	S	S
31						1	2
32	3	4	5	6	7	8	9
33	10	11	12	13	14	15	16
34	17	18	19	20	21	22	23
35	24	25	26	27	28	29	30
36	31						

September

	M	T	W	T	F	S	S
36		1	2	3	4	5	6
37	7	8	9	10	11	12	13
38	14	15	16	17	18	19	20
39	21	22	23	24	25	26	27
40	28	29	30				

October

	M	T	W	T	F	S	S
40				1	2	3	4
41	5	6	7	8	9	10	11
42	12	13	14	15	16	17	18
43	19	20	21	22	23	24	25
44	26	27	28	29	30	31	

November

	M	T	W	T	F	S	S
44							1
45	2	3	4	5	6	7	8
46	9	10	11	12	13	14	15
47	16	17	18	19	20	21	22
48	23	24	25	26	27	28	29
49	30						

December

	M	T	W	T	F	S	S
49		1	2	3	4	5	6
50	7	8	9	10	11	12	13
51	14	15	16	17	18	19	20
52	21	22	23	24	25	26	27
53	28	29	30	31			

UK Holiday   Scotland Holiday   N. Ireland Holiday   Not in Scotland

CALENDAR 1999

January

	M	T	W	T	F	S	S
1					1	2	3
2	4	5	6	7	8	9	10
3	11	12	13	14	15	16	17
4	18	19	20	21	22	23	24
5	25	26	27	28	29	30	31

February

	M	T	W	T	F	S	S
6	1	2	3	4	5	6	7
7	8	9	10	11	12	13	14
8	15	16	17	18	19	20	21
9	22	23	24	25	26	27	28

March

	M	T	W	T	F	S	S
10	1	2	3	4	5	6	7
11	8	9	10	11	12	13	14
12	15	16	17	18	19	20	21
13	22	23	24	25	26	27	28
14	29	30	31				

April

	M	T	W	T	F	S	S
14				1	2	3	4
15	5	6	7	8	9	10	11
16	12	13	14	15	16	17	18
17	19	20	21	22	23	24	25
18	26	27	28	29	30		

May

	M	T	W	T	F	S	S
18						1	2
19	3	4	5	6	7	8	9
20	10	11	12	13	14	15	16
21	17	18	19	20	21	22	23
22	24	25	26	27	28	29	30
23	31						

June

	M	T	W	T	F	S	S
23		1	2	3	4	5	6
24	7	8	9	10	11	12	13
25	14	15	16	17	18	19	20
26	21	22	23	24	25	26	27
27	28	29	30				

July

	M	T	W	T	F	S	S
27				1	2	3	4
28	5	6	7	8	9	10	11
29	12	13	14	15	16	17	18
30	19	20	21	22	23	24	25
31	26	27	28	29	30	31	

August

	M	T	W	T	F	S	S
31							1
32	2	3	4	5	6	7	8
33	9	10	11	12	13	14	15
34	16	17	18	19	20	21	22
35	23	24	25	26	27	28	29
36	30	31					

September

	M	T	W	T	F	S	S
36			1	2	3	4	5
37	6	7	8	9	10	11	12
38	13	14	15	16	17	18	19
39	20	21	22	23	24	25	26
40	27	28	29	30			

October

	M	T	W	T	F	S	S
40					1	2	3
41	4	5	6	7	8	9	10
42	11	12	13	14	15	16	17
43	18	19	20	21	22	23	24
44	25	26	27	28	29	30	31

November

	M	T	W	T	F	S	S
45	1	2	3	4	5	6	7
46	8	9	10	11	12	13	14
47	15	16	17	18	19	20	21
48	22	23	24	25	26	27	28
49	29	30					

December

	M	T	W	T	F	S	S
49			1	2	3	4	5
50	6	7	8	9	10	11	12
51	13	14	15	16	17	18	19
52	20	21	22	23	24	25	26
53	27	28	29	30	31		

Monday June 29 1998

Tuesday June 30 1998

Wednesday July 1 1998

Thursday July 2 1998

Friday July 3 1998

Saturday July 4 1998

Sunday July 5 1998

Monday July 6 1998

Tuesday July 7 1998

Wednesday July 8 1998

Thursday July 9 1998

Friday July 10 1998

Saturday July 11 1998

Sunday July 12 1998

New Season, new Football League club. Macclesfield Town finally started a football season in the Third Division. Refused entry two years previously, the Silkmen began their first professional campaign with a home game against Torquay United on 9 August 1997. Nigerian striker Efe Sodje became the first Macc player to score in the league after six minutes and 27 seconds, powering home an unstoppable shot from four yards! The Maccs went on to win the game 2–1, and were soon installed as sixth favourites (at a healthy 14/1 bet) to win the Third Division. Manager Sammy MacIlroy hailed the victory as 'satisfying'. The crowd of 3,367 was more vocal with their pleasure, singing at the ground for half an hour following the final whistle.

ACTION IMAGES

From Nigeria with scores: unstoppable Macc Efe Sodje

At the other end of the scale, Brighton and Hove Albion started their campaign against Swansea City. The Sussex club, who narrowly avoided both relegation from the League and bankruptcy at the end of the 1996-97 season, were ordered by the FA to play their home games away from the Goldstone ground during the coming season. Supporters faced a round trip of 140 miles to see the Seagulls play at Gillingham's Priestfield Stadium, and many boycotted the preseason friendlies played there. The independent supporters' association challenged the board to find a closer, more permanent home, but their pleas seemed to fall on deaf ears.

'Give us a new home', say demonstrating Brighton and Hove Albion supporters

ALLSPORT

Monday July 13 1998

Tuesday July 14 1998

Wednesday July 15 1998

Thursday July 16 1998

Friday July 17 1998

Saturday July 18 1998

Sunday July 19 1998

Monday July 20 1998

Tuesday July 21 1998

Wednesday July 22 1998

Thursday July 23 1998

Friday July 24 1998

Saturday July 25 1998

Sunday July 26 1998

Peterborough United played host to First Division Portsmouth in the first round of the Coca-Cola Cup on 12 August. An entertaining game, with Posh coming from behind twice to finish at 2–2, was marred by a 21-man brawl towards the end of the second half. Portsmouth striker Hamilton Thorp bundled Posh keeper Mark Tyler into the net to put Pompey 2–1 up. In the ensuing mayhem, only the Portsmouth keeper seemed uninvolved in the fracas. Scott Houghton (Peterborough) and David Waterman (Portsmouth) were sent off following the incident. Peterborough equalised soon after through Martin Carruthers.

ALLSPORT

Scunthorpe's Craig Shakespeare in a pre-season warm-up against Leicester

And on the same day another Third Division giant killing in the Coca-Cola Cup! Mansfield Town beat First Division Stockport County (the previous season's semi-finalists in the competition) by 4–2, following a remarkable four-minute hat-trick by Mansfield's Lyesden Christie. His goals came either side of half-time, and were the fastest hat-trick in the history of the competition. Stockport's misery was complete when their experienced defender Jim Gannon put through his own goal to give Mansfield a famous victory.

Macclesfield's Efetobor Sodje clashes with Craig Maskell of Brighton on 16/8/97

Monday July 27 1998

Tuesday July 28 1998

Wednesday July 29 1998

Thursday July 30 1998

Friday July 31 1998

Saturday August 1 1998

Sunday August 2 1998

Monday August 3 1998

Tuesday August 4 1998

Wednesday August 5 1998

Thursday August 6 1998

Friday August 7 1998

Saturday August 8 1998

Brighton & Hove Albion at Carlisle United

Sunday August 9 1998

Mid- August, Leyton Orient Chairman, Barry Hearn, decided to rename the 'O's ground after his snooker empire. What was once called Brisbane Road is now named the Matchroom Stadium. Some Orient fans were appalled, and vowed to still call their home by its old name. No one quite knows why the chairman renamed the ground, although the club's unofficial website alludes to both the legendary ego of the man concerned, and his equally legendary financial wizardry. Though why a change of name should produce tax benefits is beyond most!

ALLSPORT

From Brisbane Road to Matchroom: Orient's renamed ground

Brighton weren't the only Division Three club with difficulties both on and off the field. Doncaster Rovers started the 1997-98 campaign £3.9 million in debt, with the club being run by voluntary administration. Matters weren't helped much with what was happening on the pitch. A week after an 8–0 mauling by First Division Nottingham Forest in the Coca-Cola Cup, Rovers faced in-form Peterborough United in the second match of the league season. They were overwhelmed by Barry Fry's side, who ran out 5–0 winners. Predictable chants of 'Sack the Board' greeted the final whistle, and neutral observers couldn't help but feel that things could only get worse for the South Yorkshire side.

11/4/98: Die-hard Rovers fans bemoan defeat by Chester City and relegation from the league

ALLSPORT

Monday August 10 1998

Tuesday August 11 1998
Carlisle United at Tranmere Rovers – Worthington Cup 1(1)

Wednesday August 12 1998

Thursday August 13 1998

Friday August 14 1998

Saturday August 15 1998
Carlisle United at Scunthorpe United

Sunday August 16 1998

Monday August 17 1998

Tuesday August 18 1998
Tranmere Rovers at Carlisle United – Worthington Cup 1(2)

Wednesday August 19 1998

Thursday August 20 1998

Friday August 21 1998

Saturday August 22 1998
Rochdale at Carlisle United

Sunday August 23 1998

Peterborough followed up their first leg draw with Portsmouth, with a 2–1 away victory on 26 August to go into the second round draw. The Posh manager, Barry Fry, put his side's victory down to a fighting spirit, and a willingness to run for every ball. Fellow Third Division side Mansfield were not so lucky in the second leg of the first round of the Coca-Cola Cup. Their opponents, Stockport County, were still smarting from a 4–2 defeat by Mansfield, and came out all guns blazing. The game finished with a 6–3 scoreline in favour of County, making the aggregate score 8–7 to the First Division side, Mansfield losing to a goal in the 94th minute.

ACTION IMAGES

Defending giant-killing Barnet: Greg Heald

Another successful Third Division giant killing came from Underhill Park, home of Barnet. Losing 2–1 from the first leg to Norwich, Barnet slipped further behind 40 seconds into the second half. Norwich's Welsh striker, Iwan Roberts, coolly slotted home to give the Canaries a 3–1 aggregate lead. Barnet bounced back, though, soon after, with a header from defender Greg Heald on 69 minutes. Top scorer Sean Devine settled the tie Barnet's way with a brace of goals giving his side a 4–3 aggregate win.

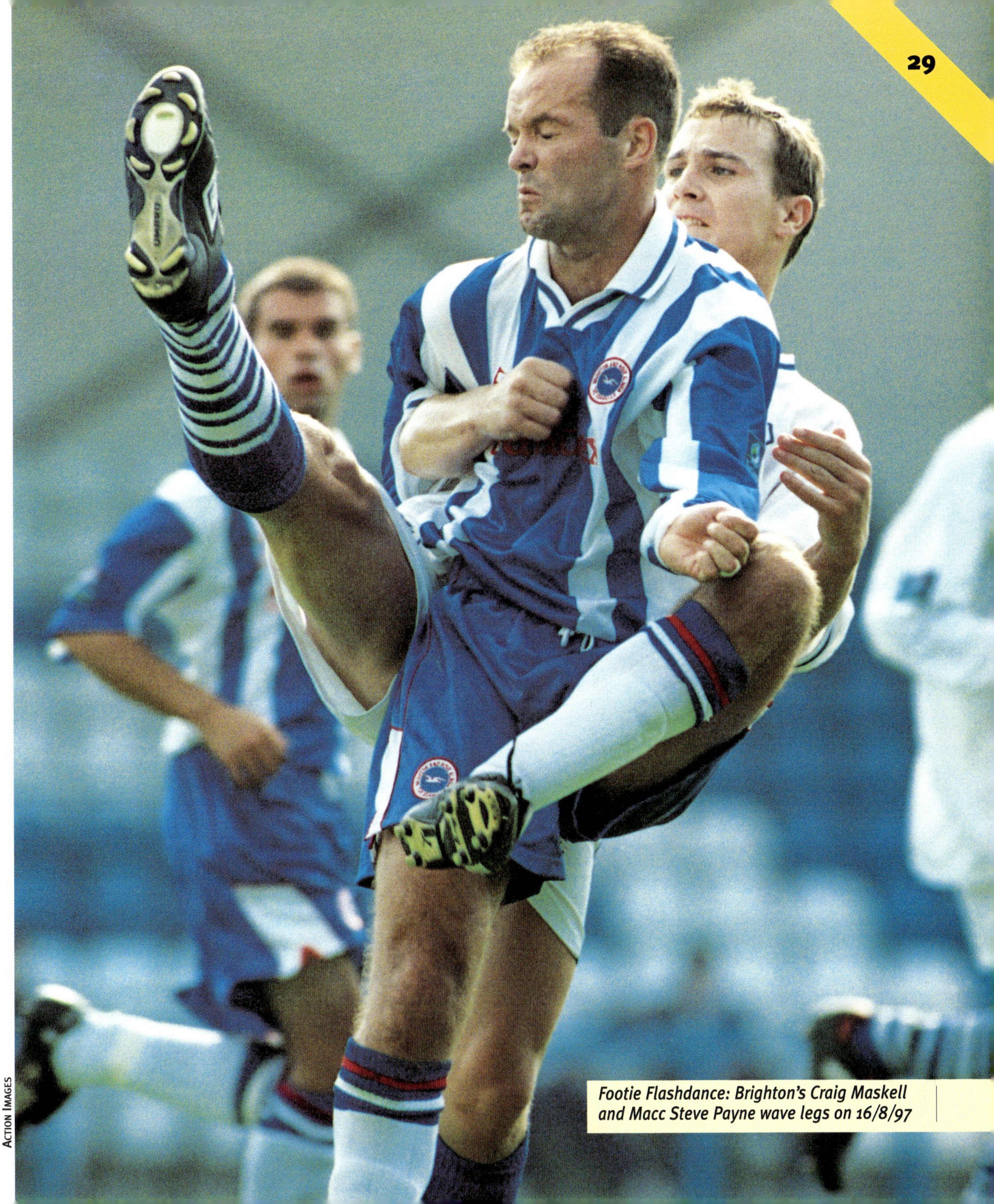

Footie Flashdance: Brighton's Craig Maskell and Macc Steve Payne wave legs on 16/8/97

ACTION IMAGES

In an innovative scheme designed to help lower league clubs discover fresh talent, Colchester United became the first club in the country to fund a programme that will see young players discarded by other clubs given a second chance to play league football. The club's Board made £50,000 available to manager Steve Wignall to set up the scheme. The aim is to track down ex-YTS trainees, discarded by clubs in their teens, and train them at the club. Many of the young players could go on to have careers with non-league clubs, but Colchester felt that many bigger clubs discard players that would perform ably in the lower divisions of the Football League.

The Devon derby between Exeter City and Torquay United on 2 September produced a predictably no-holds-barred tussle, with Exeter running out 2–1 winners. The winning goals came from former Torquay striker Darren Rowbotham who kept Exeter on top of the Third Division. As befits a derby game, there were six bookings and two sendings off, with Torquay midfielder Paul Mitchell the first to go a minute into the second half. The referee soon evened the sides up again with the dismissal of Exeter's Andy Cyrus for a second bookable offence in the 69th minute. Torquay were unlucky not to equalise, hitting the bar three times within 10 minutes, but Exeter held on to consolidate their position at the top.

Winning 3–1: Barnet top scorer Devine against Newman of Norwich, 26/8/97

ACTION IMAGES

Very Posh: Peterborough cheer their Coca-Cola Cup away win over Portsmouth on 26/8/97

Quiz 1 About Carlisle United

1 How were Carlisle first known?
- a) Shaddongate Albion
- b) Shaddongate United
- c) Shaddongate City

2 When did Carlisle win promotion to Division One?
- a) 1973
- b) 1974
- c) 1975

3 How much did Carlisle get for Paul Murray in 1996?
- a) £350,000
- b) £550,000
- c) £750,000

Peterborough Citizen

4 Who is Carlisle's most-capped player?
- a) Eric Welsh
- b) Kona Hislop
- c) Jimmy McConnell

5 How close is the nearest other League ground to Brunton Park?
- a) 58 miles to Newcastle
- b) 68 miles to Newcastle
- c) 68 miles to Sunderland

6 In which year did Carlisle win the Division Three Championship?
- a) 1990
- b) 1991
- c) 1992

7 How old was Ivor Broadis when he became player-manager in 1946?
- a) 43
- b) 33
- c) 23

8 What is Carlisle's record FA Cup victory?
- a) 6–0 over Shepshed Dynamo in 1996
- b) 8–0 over Hartlepool United in 1928
- c) 11–1 over Hull City in 1939

9 Who is Carlisle's all-time record goalscorer?
- a) Jimmy McIlroy
- b) Jimmy McConnell
- c) Jimmy MacPherson

10 When did Carlisle become a limited company?
- a) 1903
- b) 1921
- c) 1993

Answers: 1.b 2.b 3.b 4.a 5.a 6.b 7.c 8.a 9.b 10.b

Monday August 24 1998

Tuesday August 25 1998

Wednesday August 26 1998

Thursday August 27 1998

Friday August 28 1998

Saturday August 29 1998
Carlisle United at Exeter City

Sunday August 30 1998

Monday August 31 1998
Southend United at Carlisle United

Tuesday September 1 1998

Wednesday September 2 1998

Thursday September 3 1998

Friday September 4 1998

Saturday September 5 1998
Carlisle United at Leyton Orient

Sunday September 6 1998

Almost exactly eight years since the publication of the Taylor Report, Darlington finally got permission from their landlords and the local council to redevelop their Feethams Stadium. The fact that their landlords are the local cricket club proved an obstacle to building work being carried out in the close season, as the ground is used by cricketers during the summer! Once the plans for redevelopment of the East stand had been approved by Darlington Borough Council, months of negotiation took place between the two clubs, with the outcome that Darlington's redeveloped ground would start to take shape just in time for the deadline of Lord Justice Taylor's recommendations. If the ground had not been developed by the summer of 1998, the Quakers might have faced expulsion from the League!

ALLSPORT

Staying put and redeveloping: Mansfield Town's Field Mill ground

Another Third Division club facing the Taylor deadline were Mansfield Town. Following a protracted public enquiry over the club's move to a new site at Portland Sidings, the Stags decided to remain at their Field Mill home, redeveloping the ground to the standards now imposed by the Football League. A new Main stand will be built, and, with the redevelopment of the North Stand, capacity at the 'new' ground will be around 10,000. Fan groups welcomed the decision to stay, with both Mansfield and Darlington bucking the trend of moving homes to 'out of town' sites.

Division Three: the most tense of them all, as a fall from here is a fall out of the league...

Northern England Newspapers

Monday September 7 1998

Tuesday September 8 1998
Swansea City at Carlisle United

Wednesday September 9 1998

Thursday September 10 1998

Friday September 11 1998

Saturday September 12 1998
Carlisle United at Mansfield Town

Sunday September 13 1998

Monday September 14 1998

Tuesday September 15 1998

Wednesday September 16 1998
Worthington Cup 2(1)

Thursday September 17 1998

Friday September 18 1998

Saturday September 19 1998
Chester City at Carlisle United

Sunday September 20 1998

Hull City's new chairman could not escape the wrath of supporters following the 2–0 defeat against Lincoln City. David Lloyd was once Britain's number one tennis player, but has made his name since the 1970s as a leisure industry entrepreneur. His plans for Hull City include the introduction of an 'omnisport' setup at Boothferry Road, incorporating not just the football club, but also Rugby League and tennis clubs. Hull would be the first Third Division club to carry out such a policy – one that has already proved successful for continental clubs like Barcelona and AC Milan – and they would be following in the steps of Manchester United and Newcastle by expanding their sport setup....

ACTION IMAGES

Big plans for Hull: ex-tennis star and millionaire entrepreneur David Lloyd

...but what a difference a few days make! Over 10,000 were back at Boothferry Road on 16 September to see the Tigers of Hull City beat Premiership opposition in the Coca-Cola Cup second round. The inspiration behind the 1–0 victory over Crystal Palace was player/manager Mark Hateley, whose header to fellow striker Duane Darby led to the only goal of the game. Hull were the only Third Division side to win that night, and the second leg two weeks later saw them go through on the away goals rule (having lost 2–1 at Selhurst Park). Although League form was to remain poor, the Tigers' chairman and manager were very happy with the result in the Cup.

Hull City player/manager Mark Hateley: inspiration for the Tigers...

ACTION IMAGES

1998 SEPTEMBER 21 – OCTOBER 4

Monday September 21 1998

Tuesday September 22 1998

Wednesday September 23 1998
Worthington Cup 2(2)

Thursday September 24 1998

Friday September 25 1998

Saturday September 26 1998
Carlisle United at Shrewsbury Town

Sunday September 27 1998

Monday September 28 1998

Tuesday September 29 1998

Wednesday September 30 1998

Thursday October 1 1998

Friday October 2 1998

Saturday October 3 1998
Barnet at Carlisle United

Sunday October 4 1998

Cambridge United wing back Ben Chenery was rushed to hospital following a collision and a kick in the head in the 90th minute of the League match against Cardiff City on 27 September. Chenery, many United fans' player of the season, was instantly knocked unconscious by the blow, and began to convulse alarmingly on the pitch. United physio Ken Steggles immediately rushed to the player's aid and an X-ray confirmed a broken collarbone and severe concussion. A precautionary brain scan revealed no major damage to the player, although a period of two months recuperation meant that Chenery would be sidelined until the new year.

GARETH FULLER OF THE CAMBRIDGE EVENING NEWS

Cambridge's Michael Kidd on his own against Brighton & Hove Albion

It's not just the big names in management at Premier League clubs that have difficulty with the club versus country debate! Cardiff City manager Kenny Hibbitt launched a stinging attack on Wales boss Bobby Gould as the latter called up Lee Jarman and Scott Young for a U–21 friendly game. Said Hibbitt, 'I think it's poor that international players are involved in a charity game when they should be playing for the club that pays their wages.' What riled Hibbitt further was that Jarman, a target for a number of Premier League clubs, was also carrying a recurrent knee injury, restricting his training with the Bluebirds.

Coca-Cola fizz: Middlesbrough's Gianluca Festa and Barnet's Sean Devine on 23/9/97

ACTION IMAGES

Monday October 5 1998

Tuesday October 6 1998

Wednesday October 7 1998

Thursday October 8 1998

Friday October 9 1998

Saturday October 10 1998

Scarborough at Carlisle United

Sunday October 11 1998

Monday October 12 1998

Tuesday October 13 1998

Wednesday October 14 1998

Thursday October 15 1998

Friday October 16 1998

Saturday October 17 1998

Carlisle United at Torquay United

Sunday October 18 1998

4 October: Shameful scenes of violent mayhem, confusion and recrimination at Shrewsbury Town's Gay Meadow stadium... not from the supporters, but from the players and referee! The Shrews' game against Rotherham very nearly set the record for 'most sendings-off in a Football League game,' with four red cards and four yellow. Observers noted that the ref, Tony Leake, had quite a good game, and that the sendings-off could have been doubled but for his leniency. Despite all the shenanigans however, Shrewsbury managed to extract a win from Rotherham United who, like the home team, had been relegated the previous season.

ROTHERHAM & SOUTH YORKSHIRE ADVERTISER

With the days of Goater gone , the new term needs more attack options

The worlds of high finance and laddish culture met at Barnet FC, as the club announced both a new £14 million stadium, and a brand new sponsorship deal with leading 'lads' magazine Loaded. The proposed 10,000-seater stadium will be the Bees' new home from season 1998-99, and will be built on the old Copthall Stadium in North London. The Loaded deal will run for one season, with an option for the following three years. Barnet chairman, Tony Kleanthous, noted that: 'This can only be good for the club and fans alike.'

Bees become lads: Barnet show off their new sponsor's Loaded magazine shirts

ACTION IMAGES

24/5/97: Northampton's John Gayle presses Swansea at the Division Three Play-off Final

ALLSPORT

A couple of days after sacking ex-Liverpool midfielder Jan Molby as manager, Swansea City appointed his replacement. Ex-Southampton player Micky Adams, sacked earlier in the season by Fulham to make way for Keegan and Wilkins, took over at the troubled South Wales club and vowed to help get them going again. Adams appointed Alan Cork and Ian Branfoot as his managerial backup, with the team lying 20th in the Third Division, having lost six out of their last eight games. The previous season, Molby had taken Swansea to the play-off final at Wembley, where they lost to Northampton.

SCARBOROUGH EVENING NEWS

Hull 3 – Scarborough 0: what of the Yorkshire clash this season?

Former Arsenal midfielder David Rocastle scored his first goal for loan side Hull City as the Humberside club beat Scarborough 3–0 in Division Three. Rocastle, with experience and League titles to his name, scored the second of Hull's three goals as the pressure eased off the Hull manager (another former ex-England player, Mark Hateley) in front of over 5000 fans. Peacock scored the first early on for Hull, with substitute Quigley netting the third after Rocastle's effort on 20 minutes, and the former Gunner could be well pleased with his showing, after his move on loan to the Third Division side.

Quiz 2 Referee Quiz

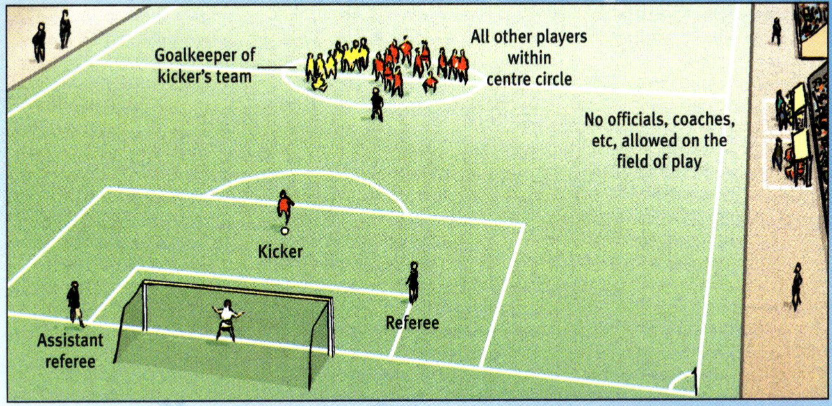

1. **In the event of the crossbar being broken, or somehow moved from its position, and replacing it is not possible, the referee will:**
   a) Allow another item such as a taut rope to be used as a replacement.
   b) Allow play to continue without a crossbar
   c) Abandon the game.

2. **The minimum height for a corner flagpole is**
   a) 1.5m
   b) .5m
   c) 1.75m

3. **A goal is scored from a throw-in. Does the referee:**
   a) Disallow it?
   b) Use his discretion?
   c) Allow the goal?

4. **Only eight players appear for one side in a professional eleven-a-side game. Does the referee:**
   a) Abandon the game?
   b) Allow the game to continue?
   c) Allow non-registered players to fill-in and continue the game?

5. **An outfield player swaps positions with the goalkeeper without informing the referee. The ref notices while the ball is in play. Does he?**
   a) Immediately send both players off?
   b) Allow play to continue and wait for a natural break?
   c) Immediately book both players?

6. **The ref gives a direct free kick in your penalty area. One of your players kicks it back to the keeper who misses the ball completely. The ball goes into your own net! Does the referee:**
   a) Order the free kick to be taken again?
   b) Award a goal to the opposition?
   c) Award a corner-kick to the opposition?

7. **What is wrong with the picture at the top of a penalty shoot-out?**
   a) The goalkeeper of the team taking the kick is in the centre circle with the rest of his teammates. Should he be standing on the 18-yard line?
   b) The goalkeeper has his arms raised when they should be still and by his side?
   c) The referee is in the penalty area causing a distraction when he should be standing on the 18-yard line.

8. **There are three minutes left in a game when one manager decides to make a substitution. Two minutes later the ball goes out of play, it takes one minute to make the substitution. Does the referee:**
   a) Blow the whistle for full-time when the player enters the field?
   b) Book the manager for time-wasting?
   c) Add time on for the substitution?

9. **What is wrong with this picture of the 'Technical Area'?**

   a) Nothing.
   b) There are no markings showing the correct distance.
   c) The distances shown are wrong.

10. **In this picture, does the referee:**
   a) Give the goal?
   b) Not give the goal?
   c) Give a drop-ball?

Answers: 1.c 2.a 3.a 4.b 5.b 6.c 7.a 8.c 9.a 10.

Monday October 19 1998

Tuesday October 20 1998
Carlisle United at Peterborough United

Wednesday October 21 1998

Thursday October 22 1998

Friday October 23 1998

Saturday October 24 1998
Cardiff City at Carlisle United

Sunday October 25 1998

Monday October 26 1998

Tuesday October 27 1998

Wednesday October 28 1998
Worthington Cup 3

Thursday October 29 1998

Friday October 30 1998

Saturday October 31 1998
Carlisle United at Brentford

Sunday November 1 1998

Rotherham United's community policy expanded to include a schools competition for both boys and girls. In association with the local Rotherham Advertiser, the Millers now give the chance for local school teams to play in a half-time competition at their Millmoor ground. The schools that enter also receive coaching from at least two of United's playing staff prior to the games being played. United's Commercial Manager described the competition as being 'superb half-time entertainment for the crowd'. With the Millers not being the richest of clubs, the competition is also useful for finding United players of the future!

ROTEHRHAM & SOUTH YORKSHIRE ADVERTSIER

Steve Thomson and Mark Monington, the midfield linking with the defence

15 October: Hull City's run in the Coca-Cola Cup came to an end at St James' Park, home of Premiership giants Newcastle United. Having already beaten top opposition in the shape of Crystal Palace, the game was too much for a side balanced precariously at the foot of the League. The 2–0 scoreline did not reflect Hull's resistance, and it fell to master marksman Ian Rush to finally kill off the Third Division side's hopes. Rush's goal, a lob over goalkeeper Steve Wilson seven minutes from time, was his 49th goal in the competition overall, which equalled the record held by England World Cup match-winner Geoff Hurst.

'Told you so!': Newcastle's Ian Rush scored to kill Hull City's Coca-Cola Cup aspirations

ACTION IMAGES

Monday November 2 1998

Tuesday November 3 1998

Wednesday November 4 1998

Thursday November 5 1998

Friday November 6 1998

Saturday November 7 1998
Halifax Town at Carlisle United

Sunday November 8 1998

Monday November 9 1998

Tuesday November 10 1998
Carlisle United at Darlington

Wednesday November 11 1998
Worthington Cup 4

Thursday November 12 1998

Friday November 13 1998

Saturday November 14 1998
FA Cup round 1

Sunday November 15 1998

The first ever league meeting between neighbours and rivals Chester and Macclesfield ended in a draw at the Deva Stadium, with a late goal from Chris Priest salvaging a point for Chester. The game was also significant as Chester had shared Macclesfield's stadium at Moss Rose for two years while the Deva was under construction. League newcomers Macclesfield, managed by former Manchester United player Sammy McIlory, took the lead just after half-time through Richard Landon and seemed on course to beat their more established neighbours until Priest equalised from 30 yards with 12 minutes left.

DAVID LAFFERTY

Steve Woods: top-scorer and top-geezer in both league and cups

A goal either side of half-time gave Peterborough a 2–0 win over Torquay to keep them top of the Third Division by a point from Notts County. Carruthers scored the first seven minutes from half-time, followed 20 minutes into the second half by another goal, from Quinn. Barry Fry's side, having lost only two games all season, needed to win to stay top of the table and keep their promotion hopes high, with Notts County recording a narrow victory over Cambridge United. Torquay meanwhile came to rest in mid-table obscurity after the defeat.

Des Linton: the kind of versatility that enables him to play down the channels or centrally

Peterborough Citizen

Monday November 16 1998

Tuesday November 17 1998

Wednesday November 18 1998

Thursday November 19 1998

Friday November 20 1998

Saturday November 21 1998
Rotherham United at Carlisle United

Sunday November 22 1998

Monday November 23 1998

Tuesday November 24 1998

Wednesday November 25 1998

Thursday November 26 1998

Friday November 27 1998

Saturday November 28 1998
Carlisle United at Hull City

Sunday November 29 1998

Just 10 days after becoming Doncaster manager, Dave Cowling walked out of the job, leaving the Yorkshire club looking for a new manager for the third time in as many months. Doncaster had had a terrible start to the new season, bottom of the Third Division and yet to win a game all season, and to top things off, Cowling claimed that the board were interfering in team affairs. He said he was told that the team beaten by Swansea would start the game away at Scarborough, so he resigned and reverted to his job as youth coach.

SOUTH WALES EVENING POST SWANSEA

From Southampton to the Swans: Matthew Bound's premiership form

October ended with a typically boisterous South Wales derby being settled by an 11th minute strike by Swansea captain Keith Walker, as Cardiff struggled to overcome being reduced to 10 men after just 15 minutes. Centre-back Scott Young was sent off for two bookable offences in a game marked by some crowd disturbances (with away fans allowed in for the first time since 1993) and the passion derbies are famous for. Cardiff still managed to dominate most of the game, hitting both bar and post in the second half, but new Swansea manager Alan Cork's side hung on for a sweet victory. Cork had taken over from former incumbent Mickey Adams, whose tenure at Swansea lasted a mere 13 days!

Former Arsenal and PFA select XI member Carl Dale wants that Cardiff scoring record!

Action Images

Monday November 30 1998

Tuesday December 1 1998

Wednesday December 2 1998
Worthington Cup 5

Thursday December 3 1998

Friday December 4 1998

Saturday December 5 1998
FA Cup round 2

Sunday December 6 1998

Monday December 7 1998

Tuesday December 8 1998

Wednesday December 9 1998

Thursday December 10 1998

Friday December 11 1998

Saturday December 12 1998
Hartlepool United at Carlisle United

Sunday December 13 1998

The first week of November saw Chester City manager Kevin Ratcliffe appear in an industrial tribunal, accused of racially abusing a young trainee at the club. The former Everton and Wales captain admitted insulting James Hussaney, but denied that the trainee's dismissal from the club was racially motivated. Chester were ordered to pay Hussaney £2,500 for 'injury to his feelings', with Ratcliffe publicly apologising for the abuse dealt out to the youngster. This, however, was just the start of proceedings, as both the FA and the PFA set up enquiries investigating the matter. Ratcliffe's behaviour was censured by the supporters, many of whom called for his resignation.

ACTION IMAGES

Centre of controversy: Chester City manager Kevin Ratcliffe

If their manager's behaviour wasn't enough to infuriate supporters, Chester fans also had to put up with an influx of supporters from other north west clubs getting into their team's home games for free! City's directors offered free entry to any season ticket holders from clubs in the Premier, First and Second Divisions. The offer didn't include FA Cup matches, and was explained away by the board as an 'encouragement to other supporters to treat the Deva as their second home stadium.' Chester supporters noted that 70 Everton supporters took advantage of the offer 'in the hope of seeing some real football'!

Chester City's pride and joy: the magnificent Deva Stadium ground in full swing

ALLSPORT

Hull has seen many changes since Mark Hateley took over: maybe this season will see them gel

Hull City became the latest victims of non-league giant killers Hednesford Town on 15 November. In a game that saw the Tigers hit the woodwork four times, they would consider themselves unlucky to be defeated 2–0 at home. Hednesford's first came from a penalty, but it was the second that lit up Boothferry Park. Gregor Rioch ran half the length of the pitch, and appeared to be upended in the Hednesford area. The referee waved play on, and Joe O'Connor took the ball from his own area to Hull's, calmly slotting past the keeper for the non-league side's second of the game.

In what must have been a nightmare for the referee, supporters and commentators alike, non-league Hendon faced third division Orient in the FA Cup first round that same day... a nightmare because each team was fielding a player named Simon Clark! Clark of Hendon was the club's current player of the year, a title he took from Clark of Orient, who started his career at Hendon before his move to Orient in the 1996-97 season! Hendon removed all confusion, however, by earning themselves a replay following a 2–2 draw. The contest at Brisbane Road saw the non-leaguers beat the 'O's 1–0, securing a second round tie against Cardiff City.

HULL DAILY MAIL

Orient's Simon Clark tussles with Hendon's Colin Simpson, 25/11/97

Quiz 3 About Carlisle United

1. **Carlisle played Darlington in the first ever FA Cup game to be played under floodlights. What was the venue for this famous cup tie?**
   a) Fleethams
   b) Brunton park
   c) St James' Park

2. **For which Premiership club did David Currie make four first-team appearances?**
   a) Arsenal
   b) Nottingham Forest
   c) Southampton

3. **Which club disposed of Carlisle in the Third round of the FA Cup in both 1993 and 1994?**
   a) Rochdale
   b) Fulham
   c) Sunderland

Action Images

4. **A club-record run of 19 games without a League defeat ended at what ground in February 1995?**
   a) Deepdale
   b) The Baseball Ground
   c) Ninian park

5. **Who beat Carlisle in the Auto Windscreen Shield at Wembley that year?**
   a) Birmingham City
   b) Manchester City
   c) Norwich City

6. **27,000 Cumbrians saw that game. What was the attendance, though, at Brunton Park two years earlier when Carlisle met Hartlepool at an earlier stage of the same competition?**
   a) 859
   b) 1,059
   c) 1,259

7. **What headline featured on the front page of the Carlisle News and Star on Saturday 16 November, 1996?**
   a) KNIGHTON: 'I QUIT' SHOCK
   b) KNIGHTON: 'UNITED ARE SCUM' OUTBURST
   c) KNIGHTON: 'ALIENS SPOKE TO ME'

8. **According to the News and Star Knighton told a reporter he once had a 'close encounter' on a motorway near Manchester in the 1970s. The article alleges that he claimed the aliens actually spoke to him, saying:**
   a) 'Don't be afraid, Michael'?
   b) 'Be afraid, Michael, be very afraid.'?
   c) 'Michael: you're going down!'?

9. **With which goalkeeper was Knighton an apprentice at Coventry City?**
   a) Steve Ogrizovic
   b) Neville Southall
   c) David Ike

10. **What happened to Carlisle goalkeeper Tony Caig on 25 December, 1995?**
    a) He broke his leg falling down the stairs
    b) His wife had triplets
    c) He was arrested during a street brawl which the police broke up with CS gas

Answers: 1.c 2.b 3.c 4.a 5.a 6.a 7.c 8.a 9.c 10.c

Monday December 14 1998

Tuesday December 15 1998

Wednesday December 16 1998

Thursday December 17 1998

Friday December 18 1998

Saturday December 19 1998
Carlisle United at Plymouth Argyle

Sunday December 20 1998

Monday December 21 1998

Tuesday December 22 1998

Wednesday December 23 1998

Thursday December 24 1998

Friday December 25 1998

Saturday December 26 1998
Carlisle United at Rochdale

Sunday December 27 1998

25 November: Cambridge United, only six places off the bottom of the League, fought back from two goals down at half-time against Division Two side Plymouth Argyle to end a run of 14 games without a win. The final result of 3–2 to the 'U's in extra time set up an FA Cup second round tie with non-league Stevenage. Beall and Benjamin scored to take the game into extra time, with defender Paul Wilson scoring the winner from a penalty. The victory eased the pressure on under-fire manager Roy McFarland, and led veteran striker John Taylor to comment: 'I don't know if we really thought at the break we could get back. We just went out and played for our pride.'

SHROPSHIRE STAR

Darren Currie: down the right wing all the way from West Ham United

Not so good news for another Division Three side in the FA Cup first round, and for one player in particular. Shrewsbury Town, on an 11 match unbeaten run, succumbed to a 4–0 loss against Grimsby. Town had two players sent off: Lee Taylor in the 50th minute for a reckless challenge, and then Craig Herbert a few minutes later for a second offence. Herbert's dismissal rounded off a miserable day for the Town defender, as he had turned a Grimsby cross into his own goal, taking the Mariners to what turned out to be an unassailable lead.

Cambridge's Michael Kidd: making his presence felt against Rotheram United last year

GARETH FULLER OF THE CAMBRIDGE EVENING NEWS

Monday December 28 1998

Cambridge United at Carlisle United

Tuesday December 29 1998

Wednesday December 30 1998

Thursday December 31 1998

Friday January 1 1999

Saturday January 2 1999

Exeter City at Carlisle United **FA Cup round 3**

Sunday January 3 1999

Monday January 4 1999

Tuesday January 5 1999

Wednesday January 6 1999

Thursday January 7 1999

Friday January 8 1999

Saturday January 9 1999

Carlisle United at Brighton & Hove Albion

Sunday January 10 1999

Shrewsbury Town striker Devon White was again the hero as his side took part in a seven-goal thriller against in-form Macclesfield Town at the end of November. Shrewsbury seemed determined to give the game to their rivals, letting in two soft goals in 50 seconds, the first an own goal from defender Gareth Griffiths. Manager Jake King, however, had built some resilience into his side, and they levelled the score with efforts from White and Richard Scott. Game over, with 20 minutes to go? Not a bit of it! Shrewsbury took the lead through White again, but Macclesfield equalised with four minutes to go. Cue White for his hat-trick, a crashing header against the underside of the bar. 4–3 final score, and one of the most thrilling matches seen at the Gay Meadow for years!

SHROPSHIRE STAR

Devon White's mighty frame hits the deck again – good while it lasted, Dev!

It's not often that there is a Lincolnshire derby match, but the FA Cup 1st round threw up an intriguing contest between non-league Gainsborough Trinity and Division Three high flyers Lincoln City. The replay followed a 1–1 draw at Sincil Bank, with Gainsborough conceding the use of the Imps ground for the rematch. Things seemed to be going well for the 'away' side when Dean Walling scored twice within two minutes to give the League side a good half time lead. Back came Gainsborough with a scorching 25-yard free kick that squirmed into the Imps net. They held out though, with Jon Whitney adding to the final score of 3–2 in Lincoln's favour. Next round saw the Imps take on Emley Town, another non-league side, with supporters hoping that they could make a better job this time....

Well, the 'Buy Kevin Austin Appeal' worked, and the Imps got the defender they needed

LINCOLNSHIRE ECHO

Monday January 11 1999

Tuesday January 12 1999

Wednesday January 13 1999

Thursday January 14 1999

Friday January 15 1999

Saturday January 16 1999
Scunthorpe United at Carlisle United

Sunday January 17 1999

Monday January 18 1999

Tuesday January 19 1999

Wednesday January 20 1999

Thursday January 21 1999

Friday January 22 1999

Saturday January 23 1999
Carlisle United at Southend United **FA Cup round 4**

Sunday January 24 1999

Lincoln City, going well in the Third Division promotion race, were brought down to earth with a crash as they faced defeat against non-league Emley Town in the Second Round of the FA Cup on 7 December. Lincoln took the lead through Terry Fleming in the first half, only to have Emley equalise, then go ahead, through former Manchester United and Wales player Deiniol Graham. The Yorkshire team, enjoying the best season in their 94-year history, looked to be going through, when, eight minutes into injury time, Fleming got his second goal. Emley had the last laugh, however, beating the Imps 4–3 on penalties in the replay two weeks later.

ACTION IMAGES

Having a right go: Rotheram manager Ronnie Moore

Who says managers' half-time pep talks don't work? Not Ronnie Moore of Rotherham, for certain. His side were drawing 0–0 at half-time with lowly King's Lynn in the Second Round of the FA Cup, with most of the crowd wondering which was the non-league side. Moore admitted later that he 'had a right go [at his players] at half-time', and it appeared to work, with Rotherham knocking in six goals in quick succession, all from different players, creating a new club record. Rotherham's victory earned them a third round tie with first Division Sunderland.

Up and up, then down to earth: Lincoln skipper Dean Walling crowded by Emley

LINCOLNSHIRE ECHO

Monday January 25 1999

Tuesday January 26 1999

Wednesday January 27 1999

Thursday January 28 1999

Friday January 29 1999

Saturday January 30 1999

Carlisle United at Cambridge United

Sunday January 31 1999

Monday February 1 1999

Tuesday February 2 1999

Wednesday February 3 1999

Thursday February 4 1999

Friday February 5 1999

Saturday February 6 1999

Leyton Orient at Carlisle United

Sunday February 7 1999

Thursday 11 December 1997 will go down in Football League history as a decisive moment in the organisation and development of the game. David Sheepshanks, chairman of the League, announced a number of proposals that would help redevelop and restructure the League in order to help it survive as a viable organisation into the 21st Century. Five plans were put forward, each given the name of a planet to allude to the somewhat futuristic (and some might say baffling) systems being proposed. Some of the options being considered included a return to the old system of Division Three (North) and (South), meaning clubs would spend less money and time travelling to away games; a 12-club Super League; and a co-option of eight Vauxhall Conference teams into Division Three.

Half of the season gone, and a triad of Division Three teams had yet to register an away win. Coincidentally all three played away this weekend against teams with poor home records. Darlington travelled to Chester, where they were beaten 2–1 (with all three goals coming in the last quarter of an hour); Doncaster made the trip to Notts County, only to have five goals put past them; and Macclesfield were beaten 3–1 by high flying Barnet. The most surprising of the three records was Macclesfield's. Since their election to the League in the summer, the Silkmen had yet to be beaten at home.

Smile of the Silkman: Macclesfield manager Sammy McIlroy lost it against Barnet

Action Images

Not much real reason to celebrate: Cambridge's John Taylor and Paul Wanless

Cambridge United succumbed to non-league Stevenage in the second round of the FA Cup. Stevenage, one of the country's youngest clubs at 21 years old, had never before faced League opposition at their home ground. The winning goal followed a free-kick for Stevenage, which was headed by United player Jamie Campbell into his own net. To make matters worse for Cambridge, they had two players sent off by referee Brian Coddington. Paul Wanless and Martin Butler (who had put United ahead after 17 minutes) both saw red in the first half.

Colchester became the second Third Division side to be put out of the FA Cup by Conference club Hereford United on 16 December. A third round tie with Tranmere Rovers awaited the victors on a cold winter's evening, and the match was typically cagey. Colchester took the lead a minute into the second half when Steve Forbes latched onto a David Green flick-on, but the Essex side's joy lasted only seconds when Hereford equalised through top-scorer Neil Grayson. The score remained 1–1 through both the second half and extra time. In the penalty shootout, Hereford scored all five, but Colchester's Simon Betts saw his effort saved by transfer-listed Hereford keeper, Andy deBont.

QUIZ 4 ABOUT DIVISION THREE

1 How many points did Brighton have deducted during the 1996-97 season?
a) One
b) Two
c) Three

2 Which ex-Liverpool player was sacked as manager of Swansea City despite taking them to the 1997 play-offs?
a) John Toshack
b) Steve MacMahon
c) Jan Molby

3 When was Rochdale relegated to Division Three?
a) 1995
b) 1996
c) 1997

Paul Gibbs: 30-yard shots from defenders are rare, especially when they get you into the play-offs...

ACTION IMAGES

4 How many teams are Promoted and relegated between Divisions Two and Three each season?
a) Three
b) Four
c) Five

5 Who fell out of the League in 1997?
a) Brighton
b) Hereford
c) Torquay

6 Which club was forced out of their home during the 1996-97 season?
a) Brighton
b) Hereford
c) Torquay

7 Which of the following teams was promoted with Wigan and Fulham in 1997?
a) Wycombe Wanderers
b) Plymouth Argyle
c) Carlisle United

8 When did Barnet win Division Three
a) 1992
b) 1994
c) 1996

9 Who was relegated to Division Three in 1996?
a) Hull City
b) Barnet
c) Notts County

10 Who did Northampton Town beat in their 1997 Division Three play-off final?
a) Darlington
b) Cardiff City
c) Chester City

Answers: 1.b 2.c 3.c 4.b 5.b 6.a 7.c 8.b 9.a 10.b

Monday February 8 1999

Tuesday February 9 1999

Wednesday February 10 1999

Thursday February 11 1999

Friday February 12 1999

Saturday February 13 1999
Carlisle United at Swansea City

FA Cup round 5

Sunday February 14 1999

Monday February 15 1999

Tuesday February 16 1999

Wednesday February 17 1999
Worthington Cup semi-finals

Thursday February 18 1999

Friday February 19 1999

Saturday February 20 1999
Mansfield Town at Carlisle United

Sunday February 21 1999

In a week of high scoring in the division (Brighton's 4–4 draw with Colchester, after trailing 3–0 at half-time, and Rotherham's 5–4 victory over Hull City both standing out), pride of place for top performance had to go to Leyton Orient. Following their loss away to Cardiff two days previously, Orient fans couldn't have been expecting too much for their next game, even though it was against troubled Doncaster Rovers. What followed was a superb demolition of the Yorkshire team by the Eastenders. Orient ran in 8–0 winners, with out-of-form striker Carl Griffiths securing a hat-trick. With a nod to Arsenal's Ian Wright, Griffiths revealed a T-shirt bearing the words 'At Last!' following the first of his three, a reference to his poor record so far that season.

ALLSPORT

Ex-Barnet man booed: Peterborough manager Barry Fry

Ebullient Peterborough manager Barry Fry returned to the scene of some his finest moments – Underhill Park, home of Barnet. Fry, manager of the North London club for a total of 14 years, desperately wanted to inflict another defeat on his old team, whom his Posh side had beaten 5–1 earlier in the season. Luck was not on his side this time, however, as Fry's team lost 2–0 in a bitterly cold Boxing Day encounter. Not much Christmas cheer for the Peterborough boss, who was also roundly booed by the home fans, alluding to his ill-natured departure from Barnet three years previously.

Where's that ball? High-performing Leyton Orient's Stuart Hicks and blur...

ACTION IMAGES

1998/99 DIARY FOR SUPPORTERS OF CARLISLE UNITED

Monday February 22 1999

Tuesday February 23 1999

Wednesday February 24 1999

Thursday February 25 1999

Friday February 26 1999

Saturday February 27 1999
Carlisle United at Chester City

Sunday February 28 1999

Monday March 1 1999

Tuesday March 2 1999

Wednesday March 3 1999

Thursday March 4 1999

Friday March 5 1999

Saturday March 6 1999
Shrewsbury Town at Carlisle United
FA Cup quarter-finals

Sunday March 7 1999

The new year saw Rotherham on a high in the FA Cup following their second Round mauling of King's Lynn. This high became a major low in the third Round, when they were crushed 5–1 at home to Sunderland. The game created two new records, one for each team. Kevin Phillips became the first Sunderland player since the legendary Charlie Buchan to score four goals in an FA Cup run, a record that had stood for 78 years. Unfortunately for Rotherham, the defeat was the heaviest they had suffered in a home FA Cup match for 43 years.

ACTION IMAGES

Four-hit wonder man: Sunderland striker Kevin Phillips

Not such a happy 1998 for the majority of Division Three sides. Football accountants and analysts Deloitte Touche announced that for most of the Football League financial matters can only get worse. The majority of third division sides were reported to be operating at massive losses, the overall figures for the division being an operating loss of over £2.5 million for season 1995-96. This was thought to have increased greatly in the following year, and it won't be until summer 2000 that the figures for 1997-98 are available. What is certain, however, is the increased financial pressure on clubs just to survive....

Scunthorpe's Jamie Forrester: losing 2–0 to Crystal Palace in the FA Cup round 3 on 3/1/98

Monday March 8 1999

Tuesday March 9 1999
Carlisle United at Barnet

Wednesday March 10 1999

Thursday March 11 1999

Friday March 12 1999

Saturday March 13 1999
Carlisle United at Halifax Town

Sunday March 14 1999

Monday March 15 1999

Tuesday March 16 1999

Wednesday March 17 1999

Thursday March 18 1999

Friday March 19 1999

Saturday March 20 1999
Brentford at Carlisle United

Sunday March 21 1999
Worthington Cup Final

10 January 1998: An historic day for Notts County, the third division pace setters. With their game against Rochdale, they became the first club to play 4,000 league matches, and celebrated the fact with a 2–1 victory at Spotland. The landmark should have been reached a week earlier with the visit of Hull City at Meadow Lane. Unfortunately for the club, that game was postponed, as was the parade of former County favourites since the 1940s. The Magpies' form so far had been impressive, making them both runaway leaders in the division as well as hot favourites for promotion. Not bad for the League's oldest club!

ACTION IMAGES

Gary Jones of Notts County shows his joy after a score

Like most lower league clubs, Chester City have to compete with bigger teams who are in the local area. Unfortunately for Chester, the other clubs are Liverpool and Manchester United! A 'Fans Forum' held on 1 February highlighted the plight of Chester's diminishing supporter base. Supporters and officials alike bemoaned the 'armchair supporters' who are happy to stay at home and watch top Premier League and European matches on TV, rather than make their way to the Deva stadium. The Chester Chronicle reported the £300,000-per-year loss that the club is making, forcing chairman Mark Guttenburg to search for new owners. One suggestion from the forum was for the Duke of Westminster, Britain's richest man, to become the new chairman, therefore giving the club the Royal seal of approval!

Crystal Palace keeper Kevin Miller fights off Scunthorpe's Michael Walsh on 3/1/98

ACTION IMAGES

Monday March 22 1999

Tuesday March 23 1999

Wednesday March 24 1999

Thursday March 25 1999

Friday March 26 1999

Saturday March 27 1999
Carlisle United at Cardiff City

Sunday March 28 1999

Monday March 29 1999

Tuesday March 30 1999

Wednesday March 31 1999

Thursday April 1 1999

Friday April 2 1999

Saturday April 3 1999
Torquay United at Carlisle United

Sunday April 4 1999

Portly Scarborough chairman, John Russell, didn't have time to reflect on his club's 2–2 draw with promotion rivals Lincoln City. An hour after the game had finished Russell, together with his commercial manager and a local radio reporter, piled into an old Robin Reliant van, and began a tour of the other 91 League grounds. Collecting signed shirts along the way, the quest was not just to raise money for the club (Scarborough finished season 1996/97 with a £160,000 loss), but also to highlight the growing gulf between the haves and have-nots in football. Russell's first worry, though, was how to comfortably fit three large men into the van. 'Think of tins and sardines....' he was heard to comment.

ACTION IMAGES

Crystal Palace's Neil Emblem battles Scunthorpe's Calvo-Garcia, 3/1/98

17 January: Another black day, in what had been a dismal season so far, for Doncaster Rovers. The long journey down to Exeter City became an even longer journey home again, following yet another crushing defeat. For the second time in a month, Doncaster conceded five goals in a game, and all hope of survival in the League appeared to be slipping away. The Doncaster supporters who made the journey carried out the inevitable protests against the Board, but little seemed to be done in terms of helping the club. The massive campaign to save the club from extinction had support from fan representatives from 71 league clubs, but unless Rovers started winning a few games, they'd be campaigning in the Conference from next season.

Scarborough's Jason Rockett: signed from Rotherham in 1995 on a free. Poor Rotherham...

Scarborough Evening News

Notts County scorer Sean Farrell: helping his team to their ninth win in a row...

In what had become an extraordinary season for Notts County already, the game against Lincoln City on 24 January saw another record broken. The 5–3 away victory for the Magpies gave the team their ninth win in a row, a new club record, and the match was described afterwards as being '...about the best example of English football you will ever hope to see!' Whether the Imps fans would agree with that is another matter! 3–0 up at half-time, the second half looked like being a stroll for County, but three goals in an entertaining 13-minute spell saw Lincoln come back into the game. Goals from Jones and Farrell (his second) put a stop to the Imps revival, however, and County pulled even further ahead in the League.

ACTION IMAGES

Fired:
Cardiff City manager, Russell Osman

Cardiff City's brave attempt to beat First Division opposition in the FA Cup fourth round came to an end after a penalty shootout against Reading in the first week of February. The replayed game (the score being 1–1 from the first match) hit the headlines for the wrong reasons, though, as Bluebird fans vented their frustration in acts of hooliganism. The day before the first game, City found themselves managerless when Russell Osman was fired, but the team put up a very good fight against a side 50 places above them. Supporters were not so understanding, however, and the violence that erupted pre-match led to over 20 arrests and the hospitalisation of a female steward. The eventual loss on penalties was quickly forgotten as the media concentrated on the crowd trouble.

ACTION IMAGES

Quiz 5 Referee Quiz

1 According to FIFA, what is the minimum length of a pitch used in an international game?
a) 90 metres
b) 95 metres
c) 100 metres

2 What is the acceptable pressure of a football?
a) 0.6 to 1.1 atmospheres
b) 0.5 to 1.25 atmospheres
c) 0.75 to 2 atmospheres

3 Is the red attacking number 10 offside in this Diagram?

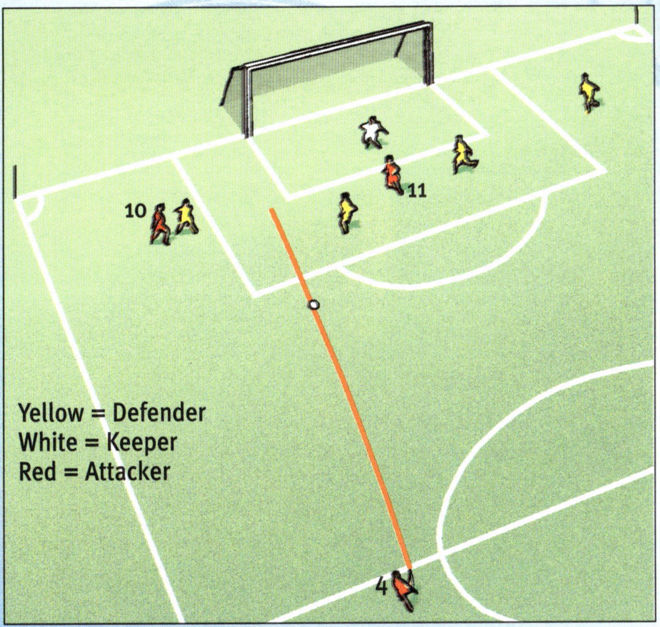

a) No
b) Yes
c) Yes, but he's not interfering with play

4 When needs to go to penalties, who decides which end they are to be taken from?
a) A toss of a coin before the game begins
b) The referee decides
c) A toss of a coin before the penalties are taken

5 If, during a penalty shoot-out, the keeper is injured and all substitutes have been used already, who replaces the keeper?
a) A substitute keeper
b) No one
c) One of the outfield players

6 Your free-kick specialist takes a corner by flicking the ball in the air and curling it into the goal. What does the referee do?
a) Awards the goal as fair
b) Awards an indirect free-kick to the opposition (the corner taker is only allowed to touch the ball once until another player touches it).
c) Awards a direct free-kick to the opposition (the corner taker is only allowed to touch the ball once until another player touches it).

7 Your keeper takes a free-kick but trips and the ball doesn't make it out of the area. What should the ref do?
a) Has it taken again
b) Allows play to continue
c) Awards an indirect free-kick to the opposition

8 An opposition player persistently stands nose-to-nose with one of your team who is trying to take a throw-in, what should the referee do?
a) Get the opposition player to stand 10-yards back
b) Award an indirect free-kick to your team
c) Caution the opposition player and give him a yellow card

9 What is the referee awarding in this Diagram?
a) An indirect free-kick
b) A corner
c) A direct free-kick

10 If an indirect free-kick goes straight into the goal, what should the referee do?
a) Have the kick re-taken
b) Award an indirect free-kick to the opposition
c) Award a goal kick

Answers: 1.c 2.a 3.a 4.b 5.c 6.b 7.a 8.c 9.a 10.c

Monday April 5 1999
Carlisle United at Scarborough

Tuesday April 6 1999

Wednesday April 7 1999

Thursday April 8 1999

Friday April 9 1999

Saturday April 10 1999
Peterborough United at Carlisle United

Sunday April 11 1999
FA Cup semi-finals

Monday April 12 1999

Tuesday April 13 1999
Hull City at Carlisle United

Wednesday April 14 1999

Thursday April 15 1999

Friday April 16 1999

Saturday April 17 1999
Carlisle United at Rotherham United

Sunday April 18 1999

Doncaster Rovers slipped to their 21st defeat of the season and stayed firmly rooted to the foot of the League. Supporters of the South Yorkshire club had been buoyant before the game, with talk of a takeover bringing in fresh management, players, and most importantly to the fans, a new chairman. Ken Richardson, the present chairman, had been the target of the fans' fury as Doncaster endured their worst season ever. A supporter campaign against the board attracted support from clubs in similar positions, and instigated a huge petition, both written and via the Internet, to investigate the 'goings-on' at Belle Vue. One question was asked by supporters, however, following this latest defeat: Just who was going to want to take over what seemed a club destined for the Vauxhall Conference?

ALLSPORT

People power:
Rovers fans on the warpath

The League's bottom two clubs met on St Valentine's Day, with both sets of supporters gathered under the message 'The Heart of Football'. Both Brighton and Doncaster found themselves in deep financial trouble, leading to massively supported campaigns to help save the clubs from extinction. Under the banner 'Fans United 2', supporter representatives proclaimed that '...football needs to be taken away from the moneymen – who take far more than they put back – and given back to the people.' The game, a 0–0 draw, was inconsequential; the importance of the day to the supporters was as a platform to highlight the difficulties of two proud football clubs.

Scott McLeish of Barnet in the Valentine's Day encounter with Cardiff City, 14/2/97

ACTION IMAGES

Monday April 19 1999

Tuesday April 20 1999

Wednesday April 21 1999

Thursday April 22 1999

Friday April 23 1999

Saturday April 24 1999
Darlington at Carlisle United

Sunday April 25 1999

Monday April 26 1999

Tuesday April 27 1999

Wednesday April 28 1999

Thursday April 29 1999

Friday April 30 1999

Saturday May 1 1999
Carlisle United at Hartlepool United

Sunday May 2 1999

A sad week for Swansea City, and Welsh football in general. Robbie James, stalwart of the 1970s side that saw promotion to the First Division in the early 1980s, died suddenly on 18 February while playing for Llanelli. Revered by Swansea fans over the years for his powerful midfield play, James made 500-odd appearances for the Swans, scoring 99 goals during his two terms at the Vetch. Alan Curtis, former Wales teammate, was at the game, and described James as being '...much loved, and one of the greatest players to wear the white shirt of Swansea'. Terry Yorath, another former teammate and manager of the Swans in the late 1980s summarised James as '...a gifted footballer on the field, and a lovely man off it'.

ACTION IMAGES

Grim: Steve Finnan of Notts County

Something had to give. Macclesfield Town, playing only their 35th Football League game, met Notts County, playing their 4,008th, at Moss Rose at the end of February. The Silkmen were so far unbeaten at home, and were handily placed in third spot for another quick promotion for the second year in succession. Coupled with County's remarkable record of only three losses all season, the scene was set for a cracking game. The Silkmen ran out 2–0 winners, extending their unbeaten home record to 20 games, but they had a couple of shaky moments to deal with, particularly a penalty award minutes from time. Macclesfield keeper Ryan Price saved well to give his team an important victory over the Division Three pacesetters.

Fighting for survival: Brighton's Ross Johnson against John Murphy of Chester City

Action Images

Monday May 3 1999

Tuesday May 4 1999

Wednesday May 5 1999

Thursday May 6 1999

Friday May 7 1999

Saturday May 8 1999
Plymouth Argyle at Carlisle United

Sunday May 9 1999

Monday May 10 1999

Tuesday May 11 1999

Wednesday May 12 1999

Thursday May 13 1999

Friday May 14 1999

Saturday May 15 1999

Sunday May 16 1999

Another South Wales derby game... and this time the police were taking no chances. The Swansea-Cardiff match is always a heated fixture both on and off the field, and the South Wales police force are used to dealing with trouble from the supporters. For this occasion the Dog Squad was mobilised earlier than usual to greet the travelling Cardiff supporters, the first time the fans had had the opportunity to visit Swansea in five years. Patrolling the skies was a state-of-the-art helicopter, catching all the travelling support on camera in case of trouble. Ultimately, however, there wasn't anything for the police to worry about. The fans' behaviour matched that of their teams, who produced an unexceptional 1–1 draw.

SOUTH WALES EVENING POST SWANSEA

Ball derby:
Charlie Hartfield of Swansea City

More woe for poor Doncaster Rovers on 14 March, as they met fellow strugglers Cardiff City at Ninian Park. Aside from losing a player on the hour mark, Rovers had seven put past keeper Davis, the last of which was an own-goal by midfielder Mike. Cardiff's biggest win for 40 years was greeted with astonishment from the crowd, although the brave Doncaster supporters who had made the long trip south hailed their solitary score with chants of 'dodgy keeper' against Cardiff's Hallworth. An inspired victory for the Welsh side, with seven different names on the scoresheet, but relegation from the League beckoned ever-closer for Rovers.

Celebration time for Cardiff in their match against Barnet on 14/2/97

ACTION IMAGES

Monday May 17 1999

Tuesday May 18 1999

Wednesday May 19 1999

Thursday May 20 1999

Friday May 21 1999

Saturday May 22 1999
FA Cup Final

Sunday May 23 1999

Monday May 24 1999

Tuesday May 25 1999

Wednesday May 26 1999

Thursday May 27 1999

Friday May 28 1999

Saturday May 29 1999

Sunday May 30 1999

Mid-March: Leyton Orient, pushing hard for promotion via the play-offs, were handed a £20,000 fine by the FA after fielding an ineligible player on three different occasions earlier in the season. What was worse for the 'O's, however, was the threat from the Football League to deduct two points for each offence. This is common penalty for the offence, and the League seemed likely to carry out the threat. Orient's hopes of a play-off place looked set to be dashed with a possible six points deducted from their total. Chair of the club, Barry Hearn, blamed the error on an administrative mistake, and the fans hoped that the League would see the FA's punishment as adequate.

ACTION IMAGES

In the push for promotion: Leyton Orient's Roger Joseph

A tense six-pointer between two teams fighting for promotion saw a marvellous performance from Barnet goalie Lee Harrison, which kept his side in with a fighting chance of promotion against rivals Torquay United. The Gulls and the Bees played a cracking first half, which saw Harrison pulling off a string of excellent saves. Barnet came back well in the second half, and the Bees nearly finished with a sting, when striker Sean Devine had an effort cleared off the Torquay line. It finished 0–0, but both sides were pleased to get a point, particularly Barnet, who remain unbeaten to Torquay in all competitions.

Busy Bee: Barnet's John Doolan

ACTION IMAGES

Waiting and hoping for the new season: John Murphy of Chester City

Action Images

A different story to last season's fixture, but a similar scoreline. Chester and Exeter, both pushing for play-off places, met on 4 April with memories of Chester's 5–1 victory of the previous campaign still fresh. Exeter, however, were having none of the same, and proceeded to tear the makeshift Chester defence apart. 3–0 at half-time, the game looked all but over, but there was to be more drama in the second period. Exeter striker Barry McConnell, already scorer of two goals, had a third wiped out mysteriously by the ref, following a powerful header. Chester's misery was made complete when John Murphy was sent off in the 85th minute for elbowing. The game finished 5–0 in Exeter's favour, and helped their slender play-off chances. Chester would have to wait for next season.

The end finally came for Doncaster Rovers that same day, as they succumbed to an away defeat against Chester City, one of only four teams to have been beaten by the Rovers this season. The 2–1 defeat consigned Rovers to non-league status for the first time in 75 years, and the game was not attended by their chairman Ken Richardson, who proclaimed earlier in the season 'I don't go, as I don't want to be associated with losers'! The Chester fans were magnaminous in victory, leading the club announcer to pay tribute to the Rovers supporters, wishing them a swift return to the League. The irony of Chester's playing of the 'Final Countdown' as the players came onto the pitch wasn't lost on the travelling Rovers fans, who all joined in.

Big Macc: Tony Philliskirk, playing against Hull, 28/3/98

Quiz 6 About Division Three

1. **In what year did the top clubs break away from the Football League?**
   a) 1990
   b) 1991
   c) 1992

2. **How many clubs are there now in Division Three?**
   a) 20
   b) 22
   c) 24

3. **Which company sponsored the Football League before Nationwide?**
   a) Bass
   b) Carling
   c) Endsleigh

Action Images

4. **Who was bottom of the Division Three table after the 1996-97 season?**
   a) Hereford town
   b) Brighton
   c) Exeter City

5. **Who was the Division Three top scorer that season?**
   a) Mike Conroy
   b) Gareth Ainsworth
   c) Graeme Jones

6. **Which pop group provides the theme tune for ITV'S Nationwide Football league extra?**
   a) KLF
   b) Blur
   c) Dread Zone

7. **By what score did Northampton Town beat Swansea City in the 1997 Division Three play-off final?**
   a) 1-0
   b) 2-0
   c) 3-0

8. **Who were the first champions of the new Division Three?**
   a) Cardiff City
   b) Swansea City
   c) Crewe

9. **Who were champions the following year?**
   a) Bristol Rovers
   b) Bristol City
   c) Shrewsbury Town

10. **A goal from Frain took which club into the Division Two?**
   a) Shrewsbury Town
   b) Cardiff City
   c) Northampton Town

Answers: 1.c 2.c 3.c 4.a 5.c 6.c 7.a 8.a 9.c 10.c

Monday May 31 1999

Tuesday June 1 1999

Wednesday June 2 1999

Thursday June 3 1999

Friday June 4 1999

Saturday June 5 1999

Sunday June 6 1999

Monday June 7 1999

Tuesday June 8 1999

Wednesday June 9 1999

Thursday June 10 1999

Friday June 11 1999

Saturday June 12 1999

Sunday June 13 1999

As one team makes the drop, another celebrates promotion and a record breaking season. Notts County, under manager Sam Allardyce, celebrated their promotion to the Second Division, and the setting of three club and two League records in doing so. The club record books were shattered by most wins (29), most points (99) and most goals scored (82) in a season, and the town of Nottingham celebrated the championship win in style. The City Council held a civic reception for the team, and supporters could have their photo taken with the trophy for a donation to charity. One sour point for the club, however, was the huge interest being shown in Allardyce by clubs in higher divisions. Magpies chairman Geoff Davey said: 'Sam is committed to this club, to the fans and the players – and we're commited to him.'

ACTION IMAGES

Wanted: Notts County's talented manager Sam Allardyce

Orient were found guilty by the Football League disciplinary commission of fielding suspended players at a hearing on the 17 April. Already heavily fined by the Football Association, the League decided to dock the 'O's three points, meaning that the East London club dropped from 10th to 12th place, effectively ending their play-off hopes. Chairman Barry Hearn vowed to fight the punishment in an appeal, but the League were standing firm, citing that the normal punishment is a two-point penalty for each infringement of the rules. Orient should therefore count themselves lucky not to have lost 6 points – but try telling that to their supporters!

Jamie Patterson of Halifax: saw the Shaymen leave the league, and now sees them return

ACTION IMAGES

Monday June 14 1999

Tuesday June 15 1999

Wednesday June 16 1999

Thursday June 17 1999

Friday June 18 1999

Saturday June 19 1999

Sunday June 20 1999

Monday June 21 1999

Tuesday June 22 1999

Wednesday June 23 1999

Thursday June 24 1999

Friday June 25 1999

Saturday June 26 1999

Sunday June 27 1999

A bad tempered affair between Cambridge United and Swansea City erupted at half-time when Swans boss Alan Cork had to be restrained by stewards as he went towards referee Mike Dean. Swans striker Tony Bird, who had scored for the Welsh side minutes earlier, was sent off for throwing mud in the face of one of the referee's assistants, and Cork wanted the ref to explain the decision. 'I don't condone indiscipline by my player...' said Cork after the 4–1 defeat. Perhaps he should practise what he preaches... and then he wouldn't end up with egg on his face!

ACTION IMAGES

Aiming to score for Scarborough: Gareth Williams

25 April: in a remarkable four-year period, Macclesfield won the conference twice, the FA Trophy once, and were bidding for promotion in their first ever League season. Three points against county rivals (and former tenants) Chester City would give the Silkmen the second automatic promotion place, and would enable them to finish the season unbeaten at home, the only club in all four divisions to do so. Macclesfield took charge, and took the lead through Steve Wood and Neil Sorvel on either side of the interval. Chester came back, but Phil Power scored the goal that took Macclesfield into Division Two, and a new derby rivalry with relegated Manchester City.

Into Division Two: Macclesfield's Ben Sedgmore and his teammates face new foes

ACTION IMAGES

Monday June 28 1999

Tuesday June 29 1999

Wednesday June 30 1999

Thursday July 1 1999

Friday July 2 1999

Saturday July 3 1999

Sunday July 4 1999

ACTION IMAGES

Fight for a last-minute equaliser: Orient and Torquay sramble, 2/5/98

The last week in April was a good week for Lincoln City, both the club and its supporters. The London Marathon annually attracts thousands of football supporters to run the 26 miles around the capital, and each year a prize is given, for each division, to the runner wearing their club's shirt. The Division Three prize went to Lincoln supporter Marcel Ostermayer, who picked up the same award the previous year. What is disturbing, however, is that Marcel was running in a Barnet shirt for the 1997 marathon, which caused one reporter to note that '...in this post-Bosman world, freedom of movement clearly affects supporters as well as players!'

Some would say that gaining automatic promotion can be a bit of an anti-climax. There's no trip to Wembley, no chance to climb the 39 steps to collect a trophy, no 'great day out for the fans' and no additional revenue. The chances are, however, that the people who say this are not Torquay United fans or players. Because at the end of a season that saw the West Country team creating a good name for itself as an effective unit, it was left to east coast rivals, Colchester United to scoop the prize and rise one step nearer to the ultimate goal of a Premiership place. Because, let's face it, that's what promotion means today. Moving from third to second is no longer a case of simply dabbling around in the lower divisions – it's a case of getting closer to the big money.

The last promotion place in the third division was decided by a penalty, as Colchester United met Torquay United in the play-off final at Wembley on 22 May. An entertaining first half produced the debatable spot kick, as Torquay defender Jon Gittens hand-balled in the penalty area. There was little Gittens could do to avoid the ball, but referee Mick Fletcher awarded the penalty, which was tucked away in off the post by David Gregory, sending young Torquay keeper Matthew Gregg the wrong way. Colchester had finished fourth in the League, and derived some satisfaction from promotion from being the highest placed play-off team. Torquay felt satisfied with the performance, if not the result, and, bearing in mind that the Devon side had finished bottom of the League a few seasons ago, the play-off final looked like a good consolidation in the third division.

Many cheers and one good reason: Notts County move into the Second League

ALLSPORT

1998/99 PROGRESS CHART FOR THE SUPPORTERS OF

		DATE	SCORE	POINTS	PLACE	REFEREE
Carlisle United ..v................. Barnet	HOME	/ /	–			
	AWAY	/ /	–			
Carlisle United ..v.............. Brentford	HOME	/ /	–			
	AWAY	/ /	–			
Carlisle United ..v.. Brighton & Hove Albion	HOME	/ /	–			
	AWAY	/ /	–			
Carlisle United ..v ...... Cambridge United	HOME	/ /	–			
	AWAY	/ /	–			
Carlisle United ..v .... Cardiff City	HOME	/ /	–			
	AWAY	/ /	–			
Carlisle United ..v .... Chester City	HOME	/ /	–			
	AWAY	/ /	–			
Carlisle United ..v............. Darlington	HOME	/ /	–			
	AWAY	/ /	–			
Carlisle United ..v .... Exeter City	HOME	/ /	–			
	AWAY	/ /	–			
Carlisle United ..v........... Halifax Town	HOME	/ /	–			
	AWAY	/ /	–			
Carlisle United ..v ...... Hartlepool United	HOME	/ /	–			
	AWAY	/ /	–			
Carlisle United ..v .... Hull City	HOME	/ /	–			
	AWAY	/ /	–			
Carlisle United ..v.......... Leyton Orient	HOME	/ /	–			
	AWAY	/ /	–			
Carlisle United ..v .... Mansfield Town	HOME	/ /	–			
	AWAY	/ /	–			
Carlisle United ..v.... Peterborough United	HOME	/ /	–			
	AWAY	/ /	–			
Carlisle United ..v .... Plymouth Argyle	HOME	/ /	–			
	AWAY	/ /	–			
Carlisle United ..v.............. Rochdale	HOME	/ /	–			
	AWAY	/ /	–			
Carlisle United ..v...... Rotherham United	HOME	/ /	–			
	AWAY	/ /	–			
Carlisle United ..v........... Scarborough	HOME	/ /	–			
	AWAY	/ /	–			
Carlisle United ..v..... Scunthorpe United	HOME	/ /	–			
	AWAY	/ /	–			
Carlisle United ..v....... Shrewsbury Town	HOME	/ /	–			
	AWAY	/ /	–			
Carlisle United ..v .... Southend United	HOME	/ /	–			
	AWAY	/ /	–			
Carlisle United ..v .... Swansea City	HOME	/ /	–			
	AWAY	/ /	–			
Carlisle United ..v......... Torquay United	HOME	/ /	–			
	AWAY	/ /	–			

	SCORERS	RED CARDS	YELLOW CARDS	COMMENTS

SUPPORTERS' AWAY INFORMATION

UNITED KINGDOM AIRPORTS

Aberdeen (Dyce)	01224 722331
Belfast (Aldegrove)	01849 422888
Birmingham International	0121 767-5511
Blackpool	01253 343434
Bournemouth (Hurn)	01202 593939
Bristol (Luisgate)	01275 474444
Cambridge	01223 61133
Cardiff	01446 711211
East Midlands	01332 852852
Edinburgh	0131333-1000
Glasgow	0141 887 1111
Humberside	01652 688491
Inverness (Dalcross)	01463 232471
Leeds & Bradford (Yeadon)	01132 509696
Liverpool (Speke)	0151 486-8877
London (Gatwick)	01293 535353
London (Heathrow)	0181 759-4321
London (London City)	0171 474-5555
London (Stanstead)	01279 680500
Luton	01582 405100
Lydd	01797 320401
Manchester (Ringway)	0161 489-3000
Newcastle (Woolsington)	0191 286-0966
Newquay (St. Mawgan)	01637 860551
Norwich	01603 411923
Plymouth	01752 772752
Prestwick	01292 479822
Southampton	01703 629600
Southend	01702 340201
Stornoway	01851 702256
Teesside (Darlington)	01325 332811
Westland Heliport	0171 228-0181

PASSPORT OFFICES

London 0171 799-2728
Clive House, 70–78 Petty France, SW1H 9HD

Liverpool 0151 237-3010
5th Floor, India Buildings, Water Street, L2 0QZ

Peterborough 01733 555688
UK Passport Agency, Aragon Court,
Northminster Road, Peterborough PE1 1QG

Glasgow 0141 332-4441
3 Northgate, 96 Milton Street, Cowcadens,
Glasgow G4 0BT

Newport 01633 473700
Olympia House, Upper Dock Street, Newport,
Gwent NP9 1XQ

Belfast 01232 330214
Hampton House, 47–53 High Street,
Belfast BT1 2QS

TOURIST & TRAVEL INFORMATION CENTRES

ENGLAND

Birmingham (NEC)	0121 780-4321
Blackpool	01253 21623
Bournemouth	01202 789789
Brighton	01273 323755
Cambridge	01223 322640
Chester	01244 351609
Colchester	01206 282920
Dover	01304 205108
Durham	0191 384-3720
Hull	01482 223559
Lancaster	01524 32878
Leicester	01162 650555
Lincoln	01522 529828
Liverpool	0151 708-8838
Manchester	0161 234-3157
Newcastle-upon-Tyne	0191 261-0691
Newquay	01603 871345
Norwich	01603 666071
Oxford	01865 726871
Portsmouth	01705 826722
Southampton	01703 221106
Torquay	01803 297428
York	01904 620557

SCOTLAND

Aberdeen	01224 632727
Edinburgh	0131 557-1700
Glasgow	0141 848-4440
Stirling	01786 475019

WALES

Cardiff	01222 227281
Wrexham	01978 292015

MAIN INTER-CITY RAIL CONNECTIONS FOR

ENGLAND & WALES

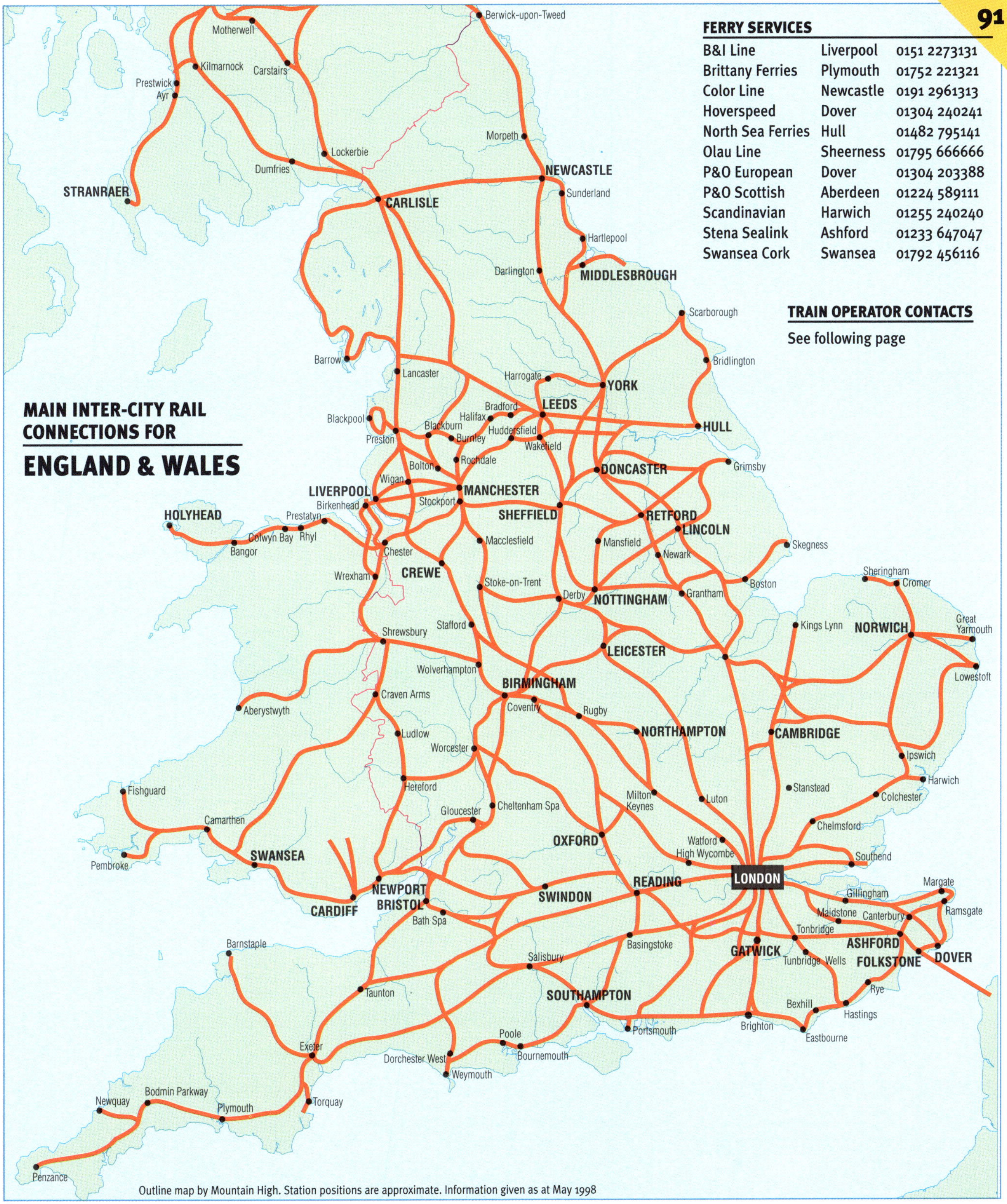

FERRY SERVICES

B&I Line	Liverpool	0151 2273131
Brittany Ferries	Plymouth	01752 221321
Color Line	Newcastle	0191 2961313
Hoverspeed	Dover	01304 240241
North Sea Ferries	Hull	01482 795141
Olau Line	Sheerness	01795 666666
P&O European	Dover	01304 203388
P&O Scottish	Aberdeen	01224 589111
Scandinavian	Harwich	01255 240240
Stena Sealink	Ashford	01233 647047
Swansea Cork	Swansea	01792 456116

TRAIN OPERATOR CONTACTS

See following page

Outline map by Mountain High. Station positions are approximate. Information given as at May 1998

SUPPORTERS' AWAY INFORMATION

TRAIN OPERATORS

ANGLIA RAILWAYS
15-25 Artillery Lane, London, E1 7HA
Tel 01473 693333
Fax 01473 693497

CARDIFF RAILWAY CO
10th Floor, Brunel House, 2 Fitzalan Rd,
Cardiff CF2 1SA
Tel 01222 430000
Fax 01222 480463

CENTRAL TRAINS
PO Box 4323, Stanier House, 10 Holliday Street
Birmingham B1 1TH
Tel 0121 654 4444
Fax 0121 654 4461

CHILTERN RAILWAY CO
Western House, 14 Rickfords Hill, Aylesbury
HP20 2RX
Tel 01296 332100
Fax 01296 332126

CONNEX SOUTH CENTRAL
Stephenson House, 2 Cherry Orchard Road,
Croydon CR9 6JB
Tel 0181 667 2780
Fax 0181 667 2906

EUROSTAR (UK)
Eurostar House, Waterloo Station, London
SE1 8SE
Tel 0171 928 5151

GATWICK EXPRESS
52 Grosvenor Gardens, London SW1W OAU
Tel 0171 973 5005
Fax 0171 973 5038

GREAT EASTERN RAILWAY
Hamilton House, 3 Appold Street, London
EC2A 2AA
Tel 0645 50 50 00
Fax 01473 693745

GREAT NORTH EATERN RAILWAY
Main Headquarters Building, York YO1 1HT
Tel 01904 653022
Fax 01904 523392

GREAT WESTERN TRAINS CO
Milford House, 1 Milton Street, Swindon SN1 1HL
Tel 01793 499400
Fax 01793 499460

HEATHROW EXPRESS
4th Floor, Cardinal Point, Newall Rd, Hounslow
Middlesex TW6 2QS
Tel 0181 745 0578
Fax 0181 745 1627

ISLAND LINE
Ryde St Johns Road Station, Ryde, Isle Of Wight
PO33 2BA
Tel 01983 812591
Fax 01983 817879

LTS RAIL
Central House, Clifftown Road, Southend-on-Sea
SS1 1AB
Tel 01702 357889

MERSEYRAIL ELECTRICS
Rail House, Lord Nelson Street, Liverpool L1 1JF
Tel 0151 709 8292
Fax 0151 702 2413

MIDLAND MAINLINE
Midland House, Nelson Street, Derby,
East Midlands DE1 2SA
Tel 0345 221125
Fax 01332 262011

NORTH WESTERN TRAINS
PO Box 44, Rail House, Store Street
Manchester M60 1DQ
Tel 0161 228 2141
Fax 0161 228 5003

REGIONAL RAILWAYS NORTH EAST
Main Headquarters Building, York YO1 1HT
Tel 01904 653022

SCOTRAIL RAILWAYS
Caledonian Chambers, 87 Union Street
Glasgow G1 3TA
Tel 0141 332 9811

SILVERLINK TRAIN SERVICES
65-67 Clarendon Raod, Watford WD1 1DP
Tel 01923 207258
Fax 01923 207023

SOUTH WEST TRAINS
Friars Bridge Court, 41-45 Blackfrairs Road
London SE1 8NZ
Tel 0171 928 5151
Fax 0171 902 3208

THAMESLINK RAIL
Friars Bridge, 41-45 Blackfriars Road,
London SE1 8NZ
Tel 0171 620 5760
Fax 0171 620 5099

THAMES TRAINS
Venture House, 37 Blagrave Street, Reading
RG1 1PZ
Tel 0118 908 3678
Fax 0118 957 9006

VIRGIN TRAINS
85 Smallbrook Queensway, Birmingham B5 4HA
Tel 0121 654 7400
Fax 0121 654 7487

WALES & WEST
Brunel House, 2 Fitzalan Rd, Cardiff CF2 1SU
Tel 01222 430400
Fax 01222 430214

WEST ANGLIA GREAT NORTHERN RAILWAY
Hertford House, 1 Cranwood Street, London
EC1V 9GT
Tel 0345 818919
Fax 01223 453606

WEST COAST RAILWAY COMPANY
Warton Road, Carnforth, Lancashire LA5 9HX
Tel 01524 732100
Fax 01524 735518

SOCCER RELATED INTERNET BOOKMARKS

The following three pages are a listing of soccer websites, some of which you may find useful to bookmark. As any internet browser will know all too well, URLs change, move or become obsolete at the drop of a hat. At the time of going to press all the ones listed were active.

If you are new to internet browsing, the following information on entering the URL addresses should be observed. Because of the way the address lines are printed, those longer than the width of the column are broken into two lines, the second slightly indented. Nevertheless, all the characters of the address should be typed in as one line, with no spaces between characters. If your edition or version of browser already enters the 'http://' characters, or does not require them, omit these from the URL address.

Where sites are official, it states so in brackets after the site name. Any useful notes about the site are given after the name in square brackets.

WORLD CUP RELATED PAGES

Football Web in Japan
http://www.nidnet.com/link/socweb.html
CBS SportsLine - Soccer
http://www.sportsline.com/u/soccer/index.html
Teams of the World
http://www.islandia.is/totw/
World Cup - Soccernet
http://www.soccernet.com/u/soccer/world cup98/index.html
World Cup 1998 - CBS SportsLine
http://www.sportsline.com/u/soccer/world cup98/qualifying/index.html
World Cup Soccer - France 98 - Coupe du Monde
http://www.worldcup.com/english/index.html

FOOTBALL RELATED

1997 edition of the Laws of the Game
http://www.fifa.com/fifa/handbook/laws/index.laws.html
Soccer Books [good reference]
http://www.soccer-books.co.uk
British Society of Sports History [reference material]
http://www.umist.ac.uk/UMIST_Sport/bssh.html
Buchanan Brigade Messge Bd Thirty-Three
http://www.buchanan.org/mb33.html
Communicata Football
http://www.communicata.co.uk/lookover/football/
Division 1 Web Pages [relates to the Nationwide leagues]
http://www.users.globalnet.co.uk/~emmas/ndiv1.htm
Division 2 Web Pages [old Endsleigh rather than the Nationwide]
http://www.uwm.edu/People/dyce/htfc/clubs/div2-www.html
England [Engerland]
http://www.users.dircon.co.uk/~england/england/
England [Green Flags England team pages]
http://www.greenflag.co.uk/te/fslist.html
England [English Soccernet - National Team - News]
http://www.soccernet.com/english/national/news/index.html
England
http://www.englandfc.com/
English Club Homepages
http://pluto.webbernet.net/~bob/engclub.html
FAI - Irish International
http://www.fai.ie/
GeordieSport!
http://www.geordiepride.demon.co.uk/geordiesport.htm
L & M Referees' Society - Soccer Pages
http://www.lancs.ac.uk/ug/williams/soccer.htm
Northern Ireland [Norn Iron!: The NI International Football 'zine]
http://students.un.umist.ac.uk/gbh/index.html
Notts Association
http://www.innotts.co.uk/~soccerstats/gallery/nmf8.htm
Scotland [Rampant Scotland - Sport]
http://scotland.rampant.com/sport.htm
Scotland
http://web.city.ac.uk/~sh393/euro/scotland.htm
Scottish Football Association (Official)
http://www.scottishfa.co.uk/
Scottish Mailing Lists
http://www.isfa.com/isfa/lists/scotland.htm
Simply the Best
http://www.int-foot-fame.com/famers1.htm
Soccer ScoreSheet History List
http://www.kazmax.demon.co.uk/websheet/tm000309.htm
Soccer-Tables
http://www.marwin.ch/sport/fb/index.e.html
SoccerSearch: Players:G-P
http://www.soccersearch.com/Players/G-P/
SoccerSpace, Football & Soccer Links
http://www.winbet.sci.fi/soccerspace/links.htm
Team England - Fixtures & Results
http://ourworld.compuserve.com/homepages/nic_king/england/fixtures.htm
The Association of Football Statisticians
http://www.innotts.co.uk/~soccerstats/
The Aylesbury Branch of the Referees Association
http://homepages.bucks.net/~bigmick/
The Daily Soccer
http://www.dailysoccer.com/
The Football Supporters' Association (FSA)
http://www.fsa.org.uk/
US Soccer History Archives
http://www.sover.net/~spectrum/index.html
Welsh Football,Football wales,faw,welsh fa,ryan giggs
http://www.citypages.co.uk/faw/

ENGLISH PREMIERSHIP

Arsenal
http://www.arsenal.co.uk/
Aston Villa
http://www.geocities.com/Colosseum/Field/6089/
Aston Villa
http://www.villan.demon.co.uk/
Aston Villa
http://www.gbar.dtu.dk/~c937079/AVFC/index.html
Aston Villa (Official)
http://www.gbar.dtu.dk/~c937079/CB/
Barnsley
http://www.geocities.com/Colosseum/Field/6059/bfc.html
Barnsley
http://www.u-net.com/westex/bfc.htm
Barnsley
http://www.radders.skynet.co.uk/
Barnsley
http://upload.virgin.net/d.penty/Copacabarnsley/Copacabarnsley.htm
Barnsley
http://members.aol.com/JLister/bfc/bfc.htm
Blackburn Rovers
http://www.brfc-supporters.org.uk/
Blackburn Rovers (Official)
http://www.rovers.co.uk/
Bolton Wanderers
http://www.hankins.demon.co.uk/bwscl/index.html
Bolton Wanderers
http://www.netcomuk.co.uk/~cjw/football.html
Bolton Wanderers
http://www.geocities.com/Colosseum/4433/
Bolton Wanderers
http://mail.freeway.co.uk/druid/
Bolton Wanderers (Official)
http://www.boltonwfc.co.uk/
Charlton Athletic
http://www.demon.co.uk/casc/index.html
Chelsea
http://www.geocities.com/Colosseum/1457/chelsea.html
Chelsea
http://web.ukonline.co.uk/Members/jf.lettice/cfcmain.html
Chelsea
http://www.jack.dircon.net/chelsea/
Chelsea
http://fans-of.chelsea-fc.com/csr/
Chelsea FC (Official)
http://www.chelseafc.co.uk/chelsea/frontpage.shtml
Coventry City [mpegs of goals... that's it]
http://karpaty.tor.soliton.com/ccfcgoals/
Coventry City [The Sky Blue Superplex]
http://www.geocities.com/TimesSquare/Dungeon/1641/page4.html
Coventry City
http://www.warwick.ac.uk/~cudbu/SkyBlues.html
Coventry City (Official)
http://www.ccfc.co.uk/
Derby County
http://lard.sel.cam.ac.uk/derby_county/
Derby County
http://www.cheme.cornell.edu/~jwillits/this.html
Derby County
http://easyweb.easynet.co.uk/~nickwheat/ramsnet.html
Derby County
http://home.sol.no/~einasand/derby.htm
Derby County
http://www.cheme.cornell.edu/~jwillits/derby2.html#History
Derby County
http://www.derby-county.com/main.htm
Derby County (Official)
http://www.dcfc.co.uk/dcfc/index.html
Everton FC (Official)
http://www.connect.org.uk/everton/
Leeds United
http://www.lufc.co.uk/
Leeds United
http://spectrum.tcns.co.uk/cedar/leeds.htm
Leeds United
http://www.csc.liv.ac.uk/users/tim/Leeds/
Leeds United (Official - CarlingNet)
http://www.fa-premier.com/club/lufc/
Leicester City (Official)
http://www.lcfc.co.uk/141097b.htm
Liverpool
http://akureyri.ismennt.is/~jongeir/
Liverpool
http://www.soccernet.com/livrpool/
Liverpool
http://www.connect.org.uk/anfield/
Manchester United
http://www.cs.indiana.edu/hyplan/ccheah/posts.html
Manchester United
http://www.geocities.com/SouthBeach/6367/index.html
Manchester United
http://www.sky.co.uk/sports/manu/
Manchester United
http://www.cybernet.dk/users/barrystorv/
Manchester United
http://home.pacific.net.sg/~jerping/
Manchester United
http://sunhehi.phy.uic.edu/~clive/MUFC/home.html
Manchester United
http://www.iol.ie/~mmurphy/red_devils/mufc.htm
Manchester United
http://www.davewest.demon.co.uk/
Manchester United
http://www.webcom.com/~solution/mufc/manu.html
Manchester United
http://ourworld.compuserve.com/homepages/red_devil/
Manchester United
http://xanadu.centrum.is/~runarhi/
Manchester United
http://web.city.ac.uk/~sh393/mufc.htm
Manchester United
http://www.wsu.edu:8080/~mmarks/Giggs.html
Manchester United
http://osiris.sunderland.ac.uk/online/access/manutd/redshome.html
Manchester United
http://www.u-net.com/~pitman/
Manchester United
http://www.geocities.com/Colosseum/2483/
Manchester United
http://www.wsu.edu:8080/~mmarks/mufclinks.html
Manchester United
http://gladstone.uoregon.edu:80/~jsetzen/mufc.html
Manchester United
http://members.hknet.com/~siukin/
Newcastle United
http://www.swan.co.uk/TOTT
Newcastle United
http://www.nufc.com
Newcastle United
http://www.btinternet.com/~the.magpie/history1.htm
Newcastle United
http://www.ccacyber.com/nufc/
Newcastle United
http://sunflower.singnet.com.sg/~resa21/
Nottingham Forest
http://users.homenet.ie/~aidanhut/
Nottingham Forest
http://www.thrustworld.co.uk/users/kryten/forest/
Nottingham Forest
http://hem1.passagen.se/pearce/index.htm
Nottingham Forest
http://www.innotts.co.uk/~joe90/forest.htm
Nottingham Forest
http://ourworld.compuserve.com/homepages/kencrossland/
Nottingham Forest (Official)
http://www.nottingham-forest.co.uk/frames.html
Sheffield Wednesday
http://www.crg.cs.nott.ac.uk/Users/anb/Football/stats/swfcarch.htm
Sheffield Wednesday
http://www.rhi.hi.is/~jbj/sheffwed/opnun.htm

Sheffield Wednesday
http://www.geocities.com/Colosseum/2938/
Sheffield Wednesday
http://www.cs.nott.ac.uk/~anb/Football/
Southampton [Saintsweb]
http://www.soton.ac.uk/~saints/
Southampton [Marching In]
http://www.saintsfans.com/marchingin/
Tottenham Hotspur [White Hart Site]
http://www.xpress.se/~ssab0019/webring/index.html
Tottenham Hotspur [Felix Gills' Page]
http://www.gilnet.demon.co.uk/spurs.htm
Tottenham Hotspur
http://www.personal.u-net.com/~spurs/
Tottenham Hotspur [check Spurs results year-by-year - just stats]
http://www.bobexcell.demon.co.uk/
Tottenham Hotspur
http://www.btinternet.com/~matt.cook/
Tottenham Hotspur (Official)
http://www.spurs.co.uk/welcome.html
West Ham United
http://www.ecs.soton.ac.uk/saints/premier/westham.htm
West Ham United
http://www.westhamunited.co.uk/
Wimbledon
http://www.fa-premier.com/cgi-bin/fetch/club/wfc/home.html?team='WIM'
Wimbledon [unofficial - WISA]
http://www.wisa.org.uk/
Wimbledon [Womble.Net - Independent Wimbledon FC Internet 'zine]
http://www.geocities.com/SunsetStrip/Studio/6112/womblnet.html
Wimbledon [very basic]
http://www.aracnet.com/~davej/football.htm
Wimbledon [unofficial - USA]
http://soyokaze.biosci.ohio-state.edu/~dcp/wimbledon/womble.html
Wimbledon
http://www.city.ac.uk/~sh393/prem/wimbeldon.htm
Wimbledon
http://www.netkonect.co.uk/b/brenford/wimbledon/
Wimbledon [unofficial - WISA]
http://www.soi.city.ac.uk/homes/ec564/donswisa.html
Wimbledon [John's Wimbledon FC page]
http://www.soi.city.ac.uk/homes/ec564/dons.top.html
Wimbledon (Official)
http://www.wimbledon-fc.co.uk/

ENGLISH DIVISION 1

Birmingham City [PlanetBlues]
http://www.isfa.com/server/web/planetblues/
Birmingham City [BCFC Supports Club Redditch Branch]
http://www.fortunecity.com/olympia/ovett/135/
Birmingham City [Richy's B'ham City Page]
http://www.rshill.demon.co.uk/blues.htm
Bradford City
http://www.legend.co.uk/citygent/index.html
Bury
http://www.brad.ac.uk/%7edjmartin/bury1.html
Crystal Palace
http://www.gold.net/users/az21/cp_home.htm
Fulham [The Independent Fulham Fans Website: History]
http://www.fulhamfc.co.uk/History/history.html
Fulham [FulhamWeb]
http://www.btinternet.com/~aredfern/
Fulham [Black & White Pages]
http://www.wilf.demon.co.uk/fulhamfc/ffc.html
Fulham [unofficial - The Fulham Football Club Mailing List]
http://www.users.dircon.co.uk/~troyj/fulham/
Fulham
http://zeus.bris.ac.uk/~chmsl/fulham/fulham.html
Fulham
http://www.netlondon.com/cgi-local/wilma/spo.873399737.html
Fulham (Official) [mostly merchandising]
http://www.fulham-fc.co.uk/
Huddersfield Town
http://www.geocities.com/Colosseum/4401/index.html
Huddersfield Town
http://ftp.csd.uwm.edu/People/dyce/htfc/
Huddersfield Town
http://granby.nott.ac.uk/~ppykara/htfc/
Huddersfield Town
http://www.uwm.edu:80/~dyce/htfc/index.html
Ipswich Town [MATCHfacts - Datafile]
http://www.matchfacts.com/mfdclub/ipswich.htm
Ipswich Town
http://www.sys.uea.ac.uk/Recreation/Sport/itfc/
Ipswich Town [Those Were The Days]
http://www.twtd.co.uk/
Ipswich Town
http://members.wbs.net/homepages/a/d/a/adamcable.html
Ipswich Town [The Online Portman Vista]
http://www.btinternet.com/~bluearmy/index2.html
Ipswich Town [unofficial - Latest News - not really]
http://www.rangey.demon.co.uk/ipswich.htm
Ipswich Town [IPSWICH TOWN tribute]
http://www.geocities.com/Colosseum/Track/5399/
Ipswich Town [The Ipswich Town VRML Site - techy, not much else]
http://www.sys.uea.ac.uk/Recreation/Sport/itfc/vrml/vrml.html
Ipswich Town
http://homepages.enterprise.net/meo/itfc2.html
Ipswich Town (Official)
http://www.itfc.co.uk/
Manchester City
http://www.uit.no/mancity/
Manchester City (Official)
http://www.mcfc.co.uk/
Middlesbrough
http://www.hk.super.net/~tlloyd/personal/boro.html
Norwich City
http://ncfc.netcom.co.uk/ncfc/
Oxford United
http://www.aligrafix.co.uk/ag/fun/home/OxTales/default.html
Oxford United
http://www.netlink.co.uk//users/oufc1/index.html
Port Vale
http://www.netcentral.co.uk/~iglover/index.html
Port Vale
http://web.dcs.hull.ac.uk/people/pjp/PortVale/PortVale.html
Portsmouth [unofficial - History]
http://www.mech.port.ac.uk/StaffP/pb/history.html
Portsmouth [Links page]
http://www.imsport.co.uk/imsport/ims/tt/035/club.html
Queens Park Rangers
http://www-dept.cs.ucl.ac.uk/students/M.Pemble/index.html
Reading
http://www.i-way.co.uk/~readingfc/
Sheffield United
http://www.shef.ac.uk/city/blades/
Sheffield United
http://pine.shu.ac.uk/~cmssa/bifa.html
Sheffield United (Official)
http://www.sufc.co.uk/
Stoke City
http://www.cs.bham.ac.uk/~jdr/scfc/scfc.htm
Sunderland (Official)
http://www.sunderland-afc.com/
Swindon Town
http://www.bath.ac.uk/~ee3cmk/swindon/home.html
Tranmere Rovers
http://www.connect.org.uk/merseyworld/tarantula/
Tranmere Rovers
http://www.brad.ac.uk/~mjhesp/tran.htm
West Bromwich Albion
http://pages.prodigy.com/FL/baggie/
West Bromwich Albion
http://www.gold.net/users/cp78/
West Bromwich Albion - Official
http://www.wba.co.uk/
Wolverhampton Wanderers [The Wandering Wolf]
http://www.angelfire.com/wv/Quants/index.html
Wolverhampton Wanderers
http://www.lazy-dog.demon.co.uk/wolves/
Wolverhampton Wanderers (Official)
http://www.idiscover.co.uk/wolves/

ENGLISH DIVISION 2

AFC Bournemouth
http://www.bath.ac.uk/~ee6dlah/club.htm
AFC Bournemouth
http://www.homeusers.prestel.co.uk/rose220/afcb1.htm
AFC Bournemouth
http://www.maths.soton.ac.uk/rpb/AFCB.html
AFC Bournemouth
http://www.maths.soton.ac.uk/rpb/AFCB.html
AFC Bournemouth
http://www.geocities.com/TimesSquare/Arcade/7499/afcb.htm
AFC Bournemouth (Official)
http://www.afcb.co.uk/
Blackpool
http://web.ukonline.co.uk/Members/c.moffat/basil/
Bristol City
http://ourworld.compuserve.com/homepages/redrobins/
Bristol Rovers
http://dialspace.dial.pipex.com/town/street/xko88/
Bristol Rovers
http://members.wbs.net/homepages/l/a/r/lardon/
Bristol Rovers
http://www.cf.ac.uk/uwcc/engin/brittonr/rovers/index.html
Bristol Rovers
http://www.geocities.com/Colosseum/6542/
Bristol Rovers
http://www.personal.unet.com/~coley/rovers/
Bristol Rovers
http://www.btinternet.com/~uk/BRFC/
Bristol Rovers
http://www.btinternet.com/~uk/BristolRovers/index.html
Bristol Rovers
http://www.cowan.edu.au/~gprewett/gas.htm
Bristol Rovers
http://www.cf.ac.uk/uwcc/engin/brittonr/rovers/index.html
Burnley
http://www.zensys.co.uk/home/page/trevor.ent/
Burnley
http://www.theturf.demon.co.uk/burnley.htm
Burnley
http://www.zen.co.uk/home/page/p.bassek/
Burnley
http://www.mtattersall.demon.co.uk/index.html
Burnley
http://home.sol.no/~parald/burnley/
Burnley
http://www.geocities.com/Colosseum/7075/index.html
Carlisle United
http://www.aston.ac.uk/~jonespm/
Carlisle United
http://dspace.dial.pipex.com/town/square/ad969/
Chester City [Silly Sausage - good history]
http://www.sillysausage.demon.co.uk/history.htm
Chester City (Official)
http://www.chester-city.co.uk/
Gillingham
http://ourworld.compuserve.com/homepages/gillsf.c/
Grimsby Town
http://www.aston.ac.uk/~etherina/index.html
Preston North End [unofficial - PNEWeb HomePage]
http://freespace.virgin.net/paul.billington/PNEWeb_homepage.html
Preston North End [unofficial - PNE Pages]
http://www.dpne.demon.co.uk/pages/pagesf.html
Preston North End [pie muncher online - front door]
http://www.pylonvu.demon.co.uk/pm/pm.html

Swansea City
http://www2.prestel.co.uk/gmartin/index.html
Wrexham
http://www.aber.ac.uk/~deg/wxm/text.html
Wrexham
http://www.csm.uwe.ac.uk/~klhender/wxm/index.html
Wycombe Wanderers
http://ourworld.compuserve.com/homepages/chairboys/

ENGLISH DIVISION 3

Brighton and Hove Albion
http://www.bmharding.demon.co.uk/seagulls/index.html/
Brighton and Hove Albion
http://homepages.enterprise.net/gjc/
Brighton and Hove Albion
http://www.aber.ac.uk/~bmh1/seagulls/
Cardiff City (Official)
http://www.styrotech.co.uk/ccafc/
Cardiff City
http://www.cf.ac.uk/uwcm/mg/bloo/biz.html
Cardiff City
http://www.geocities.com/Colosseum/1943/
Cardiff City
http://ds.dial.pipex.com/m4morris/ccafc.htm
Chester City
http://www.sillysausage.demon.co.uk/others.htm
Halifax Town
http://www.geocities.com/Colosseum/Stadium/3043/
Halifax Town [Aussie Style]
http://expage.com/page/Shaymen
Halifax Town [Shaymen]
http://www.shaymen.clara.net/shaymen.html
Hull City
http://www.demon.co.uk/Vox/hullcity/hullcity.html
Hull City
http://www.hullcity.demon.co.uk/
Leyton Orient (Official -OriNet)
http://www.matchroom.com/orient/
Leyton Orient [WebOrient - Global Orient Website]
http://www.web-orient.clara.net/
Macclesfield Town
http://www.cs.man.ac.uk/~griffitm/macctown/
Mansfield Town
http://www.footballnews.co.uk/clubs/1068/home.htm
Notts County
http://home.sol.no/~benn/magpienet/
Notts County
http://www.nbs.ntu.ac.uk/Staff/baylidj/ncfc.htm
Notts County
http://www.nbs.ntu.ac.uk/Staff/baylidj/ncfc.htm
Notts County
http://www.athene.net/soccercity/europe/eng/nc.htm
Notts County
http://www.imsport.co.uk/imsport/ims/tt/032/032.html
Scunthorpe United [The Iron Network]
http://www.fortunecity.com/wembley/villa/56/index.html
Scunthorpe United [Mailing List]
http://www.isfa.com/isfa/lists/scunthorpe/
Scunthorpe United [Iron World]
http://freespace.virgin.net/su.fc/
Shrewsbury Town
http://www.netlink.co.uk/users/ian/shrews/shrews.html
Shrewsbury Town
http://www.shrewsburytown.co.uk/
Swansea City
http://homepages.enterprise.net/gmartin/
Swansea City
http://homepages.enterprise.net/gmartin/indexnf.html

SCOTTISH PREMIER LEAGUE

Aberdeen - Official
http://www.afc.co.uk/site/
Aberdeen
http://homepages.enterprise.net/howburn/
Aberdeen
http://www.web13.co.uk/dons/
Aberdeen
http://www.raik.grid9.net/dons/
Aberdeen
http://www.raik.demon.co.uk/dons/
Aberdeen
http://freespace.virgin.net/a.morrison/ajm/afchome2.htm
Celtic (Official)
http://www.celticfc.co.uk/presecurity2.html
Celtic
http://www.erols.com/gbrown/dccelts.htm
Celtic
http://www.presence.co.uk/soccer/pages/history.html
Dundee United
http://www.algonet.se/~snoe/dfc/
Dundee United
http://www.arabland.demon.co.uk/news.htm
Dunfermline Athletic
http://www.webadvertising.co.uk/wwwboard/pars2/
Dunfermline Athletic [Soccernet]
http://www.soccernet.com/scottish/dafc/index.html
Dunfermline Athletic
http://www.aiai.ed.ac.uk/~wth/dunfermline/dunfermline.html
Heart of Midlothian (Official)
http://www.heartsfc.co.uk/
Heart of Midlothian [No Idle Talk - okay]
http://web.ukonline.co.uk/Members/grant.thorburn/nit1.htm
Heart of Midlothian
http://jambos.aurdev.com/update.html
Heart of Midlothian [has a squad list. USA]
http://www.geocities.com/Colosseum/Arena/2659/
Heart of Midlothian [Electronic Jam Tart]
http://www.ednet.co.uk/~ricw/
Heart of Midlothian [M'chester Hearts fans]
http://www.rigor.demon.co.uk/manheart.htm
Heart of Midlothian [OrwellHeartsSC]
http://members.aol.com/orwellhsc/orwellhearts/index.html
Heart of Midlothian [Midlands Hearts]
http://members.aol.com/gsha27/midlandhearts1.htm
Heart of Midlothian [Hearts Supporters USA - not very informative]
http://jambos.aurdev.com/
Heart of Midlothian [Always The Bridesmaid]
http://ourworld.compuserve.com/homepages/a_macdougall_and_ATB/
Heart of Midlothian [Rainbow Hearts S.C. Homepage]
http://ourworld.compuserve.com/homepages/andy_rainbow_hearts/
Kilmarnock
http://homepages.enterprise.net/wallace/
Kilmarnock
http://www.enterprise.net/kilmarnockfc/index.htm
Motherwell
http://www.isfa.com/server/web/motherwell/
Rangers (Official) [you need to register]
http://www.rangers.co.uk/channels/
Rangers
http://www.ukfootballpages.com/rangers/
Rangers
http://www.cee.hw.ac.uk/~johnc/Rangers/homepage.html
Rangers
http://www.geocities.com/Tokyo/Flats/5554/home.html
Rangers
http://www.geocities.com/Colosseum/Field/2968/
Rangers
http://dspace.dial.pipex.com/x-static/rangers.htm
Rangers
http://www.sgwoozy.force9.co.uk/rangers.html
Rangers
http://www.geocities.com/Colosseum/Track/7990/
Rangers
http://members.aol.com/broxinet/index.html

WEBSITE NOTES

WIN A FREE FOOTBALL BOOK!

Thank-you for buying a copy of our soccer yearbooks, covering all teams in the English Premiership, Scottish Premiership, and English Divisions 1, 2 and 3. We hope that you are happy with your purchase.

This unique collection of yearbooks, gives each supporter in the land their own club diary, supported by all-action shots from the greatest highlights of the last season, plus a diary from July 1998 – June 1999, detailing all club fixtures for the season.

If you would like to be kept informed of other football titles and next season's yearbooks, please cut out and complete this form and mail it back to me: Sharon Pitcher – Marketing Manager, Parragon, 13 Whiteladies Road, Bristol, BS8 1PB. Ten Lucky respondents will receive a free football book for their trouble!

Name of Favourite Team(s) ....

....

Name of Local Team(s) ....

....

Where did you buy this book? ....

Your Name: ....

Street: ....

Town: ....

County: ....

Postcode: ....

Email: ....

❑ Yes – please keep me informed of other football titles, plus next season's football yearbooks.

This information is being collected on behalf of Parragon Book Services Ltd.

For office use only